Praise for
Earn Your Seat on a Corporate Board

"All the best advice—all in one place."

—*John Berra, past Chairman of Emerson Process Management, current board member of Ryder System, Inc. (NYSE: R) and National Instruments (NASDAQ: NATI)*

"Jill Griffin's newest work serves as a compelling guide for those seeking positions of high service on corporate boards. She carefully highlights important nuances of the role and identifies how leaders of various stripes can effectively deploy their talents in this arena. As one who has seen the good and the not-so-good of corporate board service, I strongly recommend this work for all aspiring directors seeking clear insights to facilitate successful appointment to and engagement with a corporate board."

—*Hildy J Teegen, professor, Sonoco International Business Department, Darla Moore School of Business*

"Earning a seat on a corporate board takes work—hard work—and the process is very competitive. Jill Griffin's new book outlines how to plan your approach and lists key critical steps to not only consider but also prepare and master as you seek your board seat. The book is clear, precise, well written and easy to follow. A must read."

—*Melanie Barstad, retired Johnson & Johnson executive, independent corporate director, academic foundation director, Women Corporate Directors, Board Leadership Fellow, NACD*

"Want to join a corporate board? Don't start the process before reading Jill Griffin's new book, *Earn Your Seat on a Corporate Board*. Jill shares advice on strategy, interviewing, positioning, selection criteria and making memorable impressions. Insight from someone who knows the ropes. I highly recommend her most recent publication."

—*Mary Scott Nabers, CEO of Strategic Partnerships, Inc, author of* Collaboration Nation, *speaker, and columnist*

"Anyone who wants to serve on a corporate board should read Griffin's book—but so should anyone else who works in business. Entertaining, inspiring, and, above all, useful."

–Betty Sue Flowers, noted academic, consultant, and editor

"Jill answers the question every aspiring director asks: 'How do I get my first board seat?' The first practical, hands-on, nuts-and bolts guide on the subject, and bound to be the best."

—*Ralph Hasson, Chair, Austin Board of Advisors, Texas TriCities Chapter, NACD*

EARN YOUR SEAT

ON A

CORPORATE
BOARD

EARN YOUR SEAT

▼

ON A

CORPORATE
BOARD

**7 ACTIONS to Build Your Career,
Elevate Your Leadership, and Expand Your Influence**

JILL GRIFFIN

JILL GRIFFIN BOOKS

Published by Jill Griffin Books
3818-A Ridgelea Drive, Austin, TX 78731

Cover design by Alex Head/Draft Lab LLC and Justin Esquivel
Book design by Alex Head/Draft Lab LLC
Book logo design by Justin Esquivel
Trademark design by Justin Esquivel

The following are trademarks of JJ Griffin Enterprises, Inc.

Library of Congress Cataloging in Publication Data
Griffin, Jill
Earn Your Seat on a Corporate Board: 7 Actions to Build Your Career, Elevate Your Leadership, and Expand Your Influence

ISBN: 978-0-9969218-0-0

1. Corporate board seat. 2. Board governance. 3. Women in business. 4. Career advancement.

Set in Adobe Garamond Pro

Printed in the United States of America.

To the Luby's/Fuddruckers board members with whom I've served since 2003. These fine directors are my valued mentors, sponsors, and, best of all, my friends.

Gasper Mir III
Dr. Judith Craven
Arthur R. Emerson
Roger Hemminghaus
J.S.B. Jenkins
Frank Markantonis
Joe C. McKinney
Christopher J. Pappas
Harris J. Pappas
Peter Tropoli
Joanne Winik
Jim Woliver

Celebrating 25 years on the NYSE.

CONTENTS

FOREWORD xi

HOW THIS BOOK CAME TO BE xv

    My board experience xvi

SERVING ON A CORPORATE BOARD—WHY I LOVE IT AND YOU WILL TOO! 1

    How boards work 2

    Truths to think about 5

    Your time is now 6

ACTION #1: TESTING YOUR READINESS 9

    The board seat audit—gauge your fit 9

    Your first fork in the road 16

ACTION #2: CRAFTING YOUR BOARD SEARCH STRATEGY 19

    Board seat "skills buckets": What are your strong suits? 20

    Four decisions to set your board seat strategy 24

    Are these stories similar to yours? 29

    Establish your board-worthy skills 33

ACTION #3: FINDING BOARDS THAT WOULD WELCOME YOU 37

    Action breeds clarity 37

ACTION #4: ATTRACTING BOARDS TO YOU 43

    Your personal brand 43

    Two essential branding tools 52

    More branding tools 56

ACTION #5: NETWORKING WITH BOARD DIRECTORS AND INFLUENCERS...... 63
    Networking rules 63

ACTION #6: ACING YOUR BOARD INTERVIEWS.. 71
    I. Before the interview..72
    II. During the interview 77
    III. After the interview 81

ACTION #7: VETTING YOUR BOARD INVITATIONS 83

CONNECTING WOMAN TO WOMAN: A SPECIAL MESSAGE............................ 91
    Women make great leaders 93

GETTING STARTED...111

ACKNOWLEDGMENTS 113

CORPORATE BOARD RESOURCES & BIBLIOGRAPHY....................................117

INDEX.. 127

ABOUT THE AUTHOR.. 137

FOREWORD

When Jill asked me to read her book and possibly write a Foreword to it, I was immediately interested because, over the years, I have become fascinated by the work of corporate boards and committed to the idea that boards can and do make a difference.

My own experience is perhaps illustrative of the journey that board work can represent.

"May I give your name to the board of Tractor Supply Company (TSCO)?" Those words, spoken to me, over the phone in 2003, by Jane Romweber, opened the door (or seat at the table) to some of the most fulfilling, challenging, rewarding work of my career. At that time, I was very comfortable in board settings and relatively familiar with the general workings of a board: I had presented executive compensation packages, acquisition assimilation plans, succession and development processes and results driven performance/evaluation approaches to the bright, successful, demanding partners at Kohlberg Kravis Roberts and Co (KKR), early in my corporate career, when I led Human Resources for a corporation consisting of 9 restaurant companies.

Similar presentations were made to the board when this same company became publicly traded. Over the years, as President of 3 different restaurant companies, I presented to Boards in both public and private settings. Other Board related experience included working with a high powered, not-for-profit board as President of the James Beard Foundation during a turnaround, serving on the not-for-profit board of the magnificent Culinary Institute of America, serving on the board and as the Founding President of Women's Foodservice Forum, as well as local Boys and Girls Clubs and YWCAs. I had served in various advisory capacities, chairing an industrial council in eastern North Carolina, serving as an Advisory Council Member for Catalyst Executive Women in Foodservice, and for University of South Carolina's Daniel Management Center.

So, how did these experiences over the years, qualify me, from a small town in North Carolina, for the big leagues of serving on the board of TSCO, of looking out for the shareholders who put their trust in elected board members? It is now commonplace and critical for boards to be extremely thoughtful and thorough about the type of experience, skills, wisdom, perspective and character the collective board needs. I am proud to say that Tractor Supply took this deliberate approach, even before the increased scrutiny and accountability of boards (resulting from the financial crisis which led to passage of Dodd Frank). TSCO was seeking someone with public company background, with experience successfully leading Human Resources and businesses (general management/P&L responsibility) and with multiple, widespread locations in the restaurant or retail industry. Jane Romweber, someone I retained when developing compensation programs in the 80's (which were eventually presented to KKR) was consulting with Tractor Supply in 2003 and aware of their board search and criteria. Jane and I had not been in touch for several years, but her great memory, ability to assess people (Ha!) and genuine desire to help TSCO find the right board member, led to an opportunity that has, as they sing in the musical "Wicked," changed my life for good.......The company, our mission and values, our results and most of all, our people, throughout the company and on the board, make it an honor to serve, to contribute and to begin my 13th year of service. Thank you, Jane, and thank you Tractor Supply. Since that initial board seat, I have had opportunities to serve on other publicly traded boards and their committees, and as importantly, have had opportunities to mentor women and men considering or seeking a board seat.

Jill Griffin has created a guidebook that serves as a personal mentor and advisor for anyone interested in board service. In an engaging style, Jill provides "board literacy," defining the language of boards, abundant resource material for further study and an impressive Board Seat Audit to determine one's fit for service. Her insights for the type of experiences one needs to be attractive to a board are invaluable for those currently seeking a board seat, as well as for those still years away from serving on boards. As I read Jill's book, I felt as though I was learning from a friend, given her talent for sharing who she is, her personal stories and her gracious sense of humor. This book is both instructional and inspirational. To have the opportunity, privilege and responsibility of serving on a publicly-traded board, one must do the homework: know companies and their specific needs from the board level; know people who can be helpful in this endeavor; know thyself. Jill's book will help guide anyone seeking to serve on boards through the growth and discovery process that can make it happen.

The work of boards matters. It matters to our shareholders, our economy, our communities and to the millions of team members who, with the right organization, can enrich their lives, families and communities. Who is on the board matters. I challenge talented women and men to consider using their gifts to impact our world positively through board service. I challenge boards to insure their searches include the many women who are fully capable and desirous of making significant contributions to the work of boards. I am grateful to Jill for writing this book. I wish I had had this guide when I started on my board journey, and I know it will help others. This book matters.

Edna Morris
Career restaurateur

HOW THIS BOOK CAME TO BE

September 2013. I'm at my boarding gate at the Charles de Gaulle airport awaiting the first leg of my flight home. I've just spent the week wandering the mesmerizing streets of Paris with my dear friend and ace travel buddy, Patti DeNucci. The experience has inspired and (as I soon discover) awakened me. I'm relaxed and content, savoring the mental snapshots from this fabulous vacation: the Eiffel Tower at night; quiet, cozy cafés with savory food; tucked-away galleries filled with beautiful art. I feel refreshed and full of renewed energy.

And then it happens. From deep inside my brain comes a lightning-bolt query: *"At this very moment, what 'work' truly excites you, Jill?"*

My answer is instantaneous: "Serving on the board of a publicly traded company."

On the return flights and back home again in Austin, Texas, I think about that instant certainty. Throughout the three years that follow, I become an "explorer" with an exciting new mission: to help others blaze their own trails to corporate boardrooms.

The result is this book, *Earn Your Seat on a Corporate Board.* In it you'll learn about seven actions you can take to build your career, elevate your leadership, and expand your influence. You'll be glad you did. Not quite convinced? Read all that I've taken away from being a board director.

MY BOARD EXPERIENCE

Over the course of my thirty-year business career, I've been blessed with a host of "highs." For a small-town girl from Marshville, a tiny hamlet in North Carolina, I could hardly have imagined, as Dr. Seuss wrote, "Oh, the places you'll go"—and, I'll add, "the talented people you'll meet!"

In looking back, the pinnacle experience has been (and still is) the opportunity to serve as an independent director of a NYSE small-cap company, Luby's/Fuddruckers Inc. (LUB).

Here are ten reasons why I relish my corporate board seat.

1. What I learn in a year of board meetings is equivalent to "renewing" my MBA.

2. I get to contribute to corporate strategy at its highest level of complexity.

3. I've been part of a board that has guided two beloved restaurant brands, on the brink of demise, back to financial health.

4. I've stood shoulder to shoulder with my fellow board members, and our shareholders, to win a hard-fought proxy fight with a hedge fund.

5. I've come to appreciate each of our business units' unique corporate cultures.

6. I'm blessed to work alongside principled and accomplished directors from whom I'm always learning.

7. I've come to be comfortable with "productive conflict" even when I'm the sole voice on an issue.

8. I've become a better listener and more open-minded to differing perspectives.

9. I've learned that my job as a board director is to coach and mentor the executive team. At the end of the day, they run the company.

10. I've come to truly prize the individualized passion, wisdom, and wit of my fellow board directors, as well as to deeply appreciate how our skill sets and idiosyncrasies unite us and keep us strong.

Fact is, serving on a corporate board has made me a better businesswoman and has matured me as a human being. I want the same for you; it's my privilege to help you along this learning journey.

Let's get going!

On set at Luby's with Al Pacino filming Manglehorn

SERVING ON A CORPORATE BOARD— WHY I LOVE IT AND YOU WILL TOO!

*"To be able to look back upon one's life
in satisfaction is to live twice."*
—Khalil Gibran

A seat at the corporate board table . . . Many leaders aspire to it, and for good reason. Board service bundles together a host of rewarding experiences, among them the opportunity to be an "insider" and view, firsthand, how another successful company works at its highest levels, and the privilege of working beside and soaking up the wisdom of the brightest and most articulate professionals who will ever cross your path.

But there's more. It is prestigious to serve on a corporate board, particularly when the firm is publicly held and directors are elected by shareholders rather than appointed by the CEO—as is the case with private corporate boards. Shareholder votes are flattering, and that appeals to someone who wants more responsibility. In addition, the board in large public companies tends to have more "defacto" power. Many shareholders grant proxies to the directors to vote their shares at general meetings, and they accept the recommendations of the board since each shareholder's power as well as interest and information is so small.

My whip-smart friend and colleague Bob Gutermuth, who consults with senior leaders in Fortune 100 firms, puts it this way: "If you think about a corporate board seat, it's the 'I made it' badge. It's a seat at the top."

HOW BOARDS WORK

As I mentioned above, the board of directors of a publicly held corporation consists of individuals who are elected as representatives of the stockholders to establish corporate governance policies and to make decisions on major company issues. Every public company must have a board of directors. Some private and nonprofit companies have a board of directors as well. (Heads up! Unless otherwise stated, when I refer in a chapter to a board, I mean a public corporation board, not a private or nonprofit one. See the box titled "Two Kinds of Corporate Boards" in chapter 2 for more details about their distinctions.)

In general, the board has a legal duty to act solely on behalf of shareholders and thus makes decisions for them. The board looks out for the financial well-being of the company. Issues that fall under a board's purview include the hiring and firing of executives, stock dividend policies, and executive compensation. A board of directors is likewise responsible for helping a corporation set broad goals and for supporting executives in their duties, while also ensuring that the company has adequate resources at its disposal and those resources are managed well.

The following information may help you realistically determine whether you want to pursue earning a seat on a corporate board.

Each public company has a capitalization (or "cap") size: that is, the market value of the company's outstanding shares of stock. Depending on the source, the "breaks" between cap sizes can be different. For instance, according to the 2014 Frederic W. Cook & Company Board Compensation Study:

Large-cap	(greater than $10B)
Mid-cap	($2B to $10B)
Small-cap	($300 M to $2B)
Micro-cap	(less than $300M)

Furthermore, you'll need to know how much time you would be expected to devote to service on a board of directors. According to a 2014 National Association of Public Company Governance Survey, your public board directorship would result in these time commitments per year (figures are rounded to the nearest hour):

Large-cap	309
Mid-cap	277
Small-cap	278
Micro-cap	248

Just as time commitments vary per cap size, so does public board director compensation. The following compensation figures from the 2014 Frederic W. Cook & Company Board Compensation Study include both retainer and stock awards. All four company size segments provide at least 50 percent of total compensation in equity, on average.

Large-cap	$250,000
Mid-cap	$189,000
Small-cap	$133,871
Micro-cap	Similar to small cap

Still more good news is that retirement age is on the rise. Spencer Stuart U.S. Board Index 2014 reports that the average retirement age for Standard & Poor's company boards is 72, and 24 percent have a retirement age of 75 or older.

And, finally, here's a sample meeting agenda from my Luby's board meetings.

Board Meeting Agenda

Day One

8:00 a.m.	Breakfast (3rd Floor - Main Room)
8:30 a.m. - 9:00 a.m.	Management Report: Results: Period 10-12 (CEO/COO/CFO)
9:00 a.m. - 12:00 p.m.	F&A Committee Meeting P&A Committee Meeting
12:00 p.m. - 12:15 p.m.	Break/Grab Lunch
12:15 p.m. - 1:00 p.m.	Working Lunch - Marketing Update & Annual Marketing Plan
1:00 p.m. - 3:00 p.m.	Management Report: Plans and Strategic Focus Growth: Capital Expenditures, Remodels and Return on Capital Structure, Excess Asset Sales and Debt
3:00 p.m. - 3:30 p.m.	Brief Review and Approval of Budget
3:30 p.m. - 4:30 p.m.	Executive Compensation Committee Meeting
5:30 p.m.	Cocktails & Dinner

Day Two

7:30 a.m.	Breakfast
8:00 a.m. - 8:45 a.m.	Nominating and Governance Committee Meeting

8:45 a.m. - 9:00 a.m.   General Counsel Report
9:00 a.m. - 11:00 a.m.   Board Meeting
                                 Approval of Minutes
                                 Committee Reports
                                 Additional Open Items
11:00 a.m. - 11:30 a.m.   Board of Directors Executive
                                 Session
12:00 p.m.   Adjourn

TRUTHS TO THINK ABOUT

For too many decades, America's corporate boards have been filled by a chosen few.

I'm passionate about helping to level the playing field and making board seats obtainable to a wider, more diverse range of talent. As I see it, the future success of our corporations, and our country's free enterprise system, depends on it.

In their June 2011 *Harvard Business Review* article "Defend Your Research: What Makes a Team Smarter? More Women," Anita Woolley and Thomas W. Malone wrote: "There's little correlation between a group's collective intelligence and the IQs of its individual members. But if a group includes more women, its collective intelligence rises." The authors and their assistants had given standard intelligence tests to subjects between 18 and 60 years old. Each team was asked to solve one complex problem along with completing such tasks as brainstorming, visual puzzles, and decision-making exercises. "Teams were given intelligence scores based on their performance. Though the teams that had members with higher IQs didn't earn much higher scores, those that had more women did."

So, female and male readers, listen up. While corporate board seats are scarce, competition is fierce, and director turnover is low, here's something to celebrate: Unlike the past when boards often interviewed just one person whom they knew, many boards are now interviewing several candidates. This means, according to the Spencer Stuart U.S. Board Index 2014, more first-time directors—39 percent of newly seated directors are serving for the first time—and people with different experience, are being invited to the process. And the 2014 National Association of Public Company Governance Survey confirms that 23 percent of all new directors are division/subsidiary presidents and other line and functional leaders. This is almost double their representation a decade ago.

So you don't have to sit passively just wishing and hoping. You can take action. In fact, the "right" initiatives can immeasurably increase your odds of landing a seat. (This book is full of examples of folks who have done just that!)

Here's the tricky part, however: Joining a corporate board is generally by invitation only. (Sometimes board recruiters build the candidate list, but many times, the board works independently.) Although the landscape is changing, direct solicitation is still considered taboo. Consequently, your actions should be carefully choreographed so that the board finds you and determines that you are the most qualified candidate for the seat. You'll want to rely on your sponsors and supporters to do the initial canvassing for you.

YOUR TIME IS NOW

If this sounds mysterious and murky, or downright implausible, hang on!

In this book I bring together my branding and marketing experience *and* my thirteen-years-and-counting boardroom experience. It's the interweaving of these two distinct sets of qualifications that enables me to help you blaze your trail to a corporate board seat.

The earlier you get familiar with the world of corporate boards, the more productive your journey will be.

Refer to the resources at the back of this book to jump-start your discovery. And be sure to take to heart the "Tools for Your Journey" summary I provide at the end of every chapter.

Ready to turn your ambition into action and become a corporate board director?

Read on!

Your someday starts now.

ACTION #1:
TESTING YOUR READINESS

*"There are three things extremely hard: steel,
a diamond, and to know one's self."*
—Benjamin Franklin

An important early step in your corporate board journey is to gauge your current readiness to take a seat in the corporate boardroom. As you realize from your reading, this work requires some special skills. If you have them, your experience is likely to be a positive one.

THE BOARD SEAT AUDIT—GAUGE YOUR FIT

To help you access your suitability, I've developed what I call the "Board Seat Readiness Audit." Over many years, I've designed for clients a ton of research audits and surveys that used some fancy measurement metrics. (Likert Scale, anyone?) But my goal was brevity, and so I've kept this audit simple! I envision someone completing this on a flight from Houston to New York, for instance.

I've worked hard to reduce your responses to the good ole "Yes, No, or Maybe," with the following values: Yes = 3 points; No = 0 points; Maybe = 1 point.

Before you begin, take a moment to reflect on your work style and employment history. Above all, be truthful and candid with yourself. (You can find the online version at BoardSeatReadinessAudit.com.)

1. Do you truly have the time to serve?

   _____

   Saying "yes" to a seat can carry a commitment of five to ten years. In fact, it's not unusual to serve for ten years or *more*. This includes attending, on average, six to eight meetings a year (and the travel time to and from those meetings), serving on at least one committee, and being "on call" when unexpected issues arise.

2. Is compensation a secondary motive for you in seeking corporate board service?

   _____

   If to any degree you are driven by money to seek a seat on a corporate board, think again. There are probably far easier ways to earn it. Board service should ideally happen when you are financially stable and do not "need" the fees or stock.

3. Are you well-informed about board of directors liability?

   _____

Officers and directors of public companies always face the possibility that investors, regulators, and even criminal prosecutors might challenge their decisions. This increased scrutiny makes it more important than ever that you understand the obligations and potential liabilities inherent in public board service.

Beginning in 2001, major corporate accounting scandals at Enron, WorldCom, and other large-cap companies cost investors billions of dollars when their share prices collapsed. This shook public confidence in the US securities markets. Soon thereafter, on July 30, 2002, the Sarbanes-Oxley Act was enacted, which covers the responsibilities of a public corporation's board of directors, adds criminal penalties for certain misconduct, and addresses issues such as auditor independence, corporate governance, internal control assessment, and enhanced financial disclosure.

Bottom line: Public board service comes with *serious obligations*. Proceed with caution.

4. Do you think like an entrepreneur?

The very best and the most successful companies in America (3M, for instance) have always managed to maintain an entrepreneurial spirit no matter how big they've become. A culture that encourages creativity and inventiveness instills in its people passion and an urgency to create, and in its leaders openness to entirely new ideas—many of which come from outside the firm's respective industry.

5. Are you financially literate?

_____

Financial acuity is an essential proficiency in a board director. While you don't have to be a CFO or an accountant, you must have the know-how to analyze financial statements. Enron's and other corporations' scandals drove legislation to ensure this.

6. Are you a natural mentor?

_____

The role of a director differs greatly from that of an operating executive who is accustomed to "running the show." Most director time is spent reviewing and assessing strategy, risk, financial reporting, and management performance. Aspiring board members should be comfortable in the role of mentoring. On the Luby's board on which I serve, we have used a "board buddy" system in which a board director and a senior executive are matched. In my case, I was paired with Scott Gray, the firm's CFO. He and I meet periodically and exchange ideas. He's taught me how to dig deeper into financial statements, and I've helped him build on his already savvy marketing acumen.

7. Can you bring valuable contacts to the table?

_____

Board directors are expected to make their network of problem solvers available to the corporation's management team. Do you have a wide network, especially in your field of expertise, and are you generously willing to share their names? For instance, I live in Austin, a city known for its software start-ups. Through networking, I came across a leading-edge technology. It allowed Luby's to survey customers via a touch-point screen strategically located at the entrance of each restaurant. This information has helped us serve our patrons better. But even more gratifying for me was that, after a year of relentless system testing, Luby's signed a contract with this deserving start-up, which moved it into profitability.

8. Do you naturally bring humor to stressful situations?

Great board members, like great leaders, have a sense of humor and know how to have fun. But they intuitively understand the rules of humor and don't have fun at someone else's expense. Instead, they make light of themselves.

Many stories told by President John F. Kennedy show the power of humor and the art of self-deprecation. The website *The Hill* shares a few great examples in the article, "Kennedy's wit and humor: A legacy for political leadership" (November 20, 2013). Dan Glickman wrote, "During the 1960 campaign when pundits and opponents complained about his wealth, he simply replied 'I just received the following wire from my generous Daddy. "Dear Jack, Don't buy a single vote more than is necessary. I'll be damned if I am going to pay for a landslide."' . . . Or when a young boy asked him how he became a war hero, he gracefully responded that

'it was absolutely involuntary; they sunk my boat.'"
That's one of my favorite examples.

9. Do you like to dig deep for insight?

_____

Men and women with this gift have a natural curiosity that drives in-depth analysis. This innate talent is prized in the boardroom. James S. Turley, retired chairman and CEO of Ernst & Young, advises: "You are empowered to ask any question as a director. You are not management. Your job is to provide governance and oversight. Outside of board meetings, there is often a lot of homework to be done with managers and understanding how they see the business and how they think. These are serious roles. You don't just hang out."

10. Are you a team player?

_____

A team player is generally described as one who communicates constructively, demonstrates reliability, works as a problem-solver, treats others in a respectful and supportive manner, shows commitment to the team, and is skilled at building on the ideas of others. Are these your strong suits?

11. Are you optimistic?

_____

An optimistic mindset enables a board director to view a conflict as a problem to be solved. Rather than focus on blame, he or she will focus on solutions.

Boards need men and women with this mindset to avoid gridlock and to move the firm forward. Ask yourself: Would your colleagues describe you as seeing the glass half-full rather than half-empty? Make no mistake: Boards want what Seth Godin calls "a generous skeptic." That's the director who can take the opposing position and help shed light on its merits. But, at the end of the day, the best boards work as a team and move ahead with an optimistic, can-do attitude.

12. Are you willing to speak up about sensitive topics?

Boards depend on directors who not only speak up about sensitive topics but also are skilled in framing their points in an honest, confident, respectful, and positive manner. Sensitive topics can range from nepotism and outward signs of prejudice to unanswered telephone calls and queries. In making such probing yet diplomatic remarks, it's especially important to show respect for the work of the team. Does this kind of diplomacy come naturally to you?

13. Can you cast the lone vote?

Are you capable of casting the lone "no" vote? Can you do so even when your vote is clearly out of step with valued colleagues?

My friend and valued colleague Ralph Hasson contributed this question and remembers the sobering experience well. On a critical vote, he stood alone and voted "no" when the majority of his fellow directors voted "yes" and one abstained. Ralph recalls that afterward, the director who abstained turned to Ralph and said, "I wish I had voted 'no.'"

Like Ralph, I have cast the lone vote. You may be uncomfortable when you do it, but you eventually experience a satisfied feeling of knowing you have looked inside your heart and stood for your values.

What do your colleagues think?

After reflecting on your own, have some close friends and colleagues take the same audit on your behalf, imagining you in the boardroom. How do their impressions of you compare with your own? What can their impressions teach you about your true fit for corporate board service?

YOUR FIRST FORK IN THE ROAD

Now, tally your points and then consult others. With that input in hand, consider these three options:

Not for Me: Score: 10 or below
Corporate board service is not a good fit for me (at least not at this time). I'm better off investing my time elsewhere. No worries! There's a big world out there awaiting my talents.

In for Now: Score: 11–30
I'm still debating whether corporate board service is right for me. It's a big commitment. This book will help me decide.

Full Speed Ahead: Score: 31–39
I'm corporate board material. I'm ready for the journey. This
book will help me blaze my trail.

When you consider your audit results, imagine yourself sitting in your car at a traffic light.

The green light solidifies your readiness to forge ahead. The yellow caution light signifies not all is "clear," and you may need to be extra careful as you drive forward. The red light, often blinking brightly, conveys the indisputable warning to stop. Each colored light sends a different signal. That's what the audit is designed to do as well.

TOOLS FOR YOUR JOURNEY

- With corporate board service comes many demands. After careful assessment, you may come to realize it's absolutely not for you. This book will describe other options for you to consider—nonprofit boards and private company boards, for instance, either of which can bring you much satisfaction.
- Always involve family, friends, trusted colleagues, and mentors in every decision you make regarding whether or not to pursue corporate board service. Never keep your own counsel. As we all have learned, two heads (or a multitude) are better than one.

ACTION #2:
CRAFTING YOUR BOARD SEARCH STRATEGY

"The essence of strategy is choosing what not to do."
—Michael Porter

In the previous chapter, you assessed your readiness to seek out an opportunity to be on a corporate board. Now that you've determined you are ready, willing, and able, there are more questions to be asked and answered.

First up, "What does the *board* want?"

That's the question ace board recruiter Jan Lehman raised the instant I began my interview with her about winning a corporate board seat.

Jan was very clear: You, as a savvy board aspirant, must first focus deeply on what the board wants rather than beginning with what you can bring to the board.

Two Kinds of Corporate Boards

Public: The large public corporations are the ones we generally hear about on the news: Microsoft, GE, Ford, Google, etc. Public corporations are traded on a national trade exchange—Nasdaq or the New York Stock Exchange, for example.

Private: Corporations are "private" because they are not traded on a national trade exchange. They are often owned by a small group of investors or are a family business. There are many private companies with high profiles: Publix Super Markets, Cox Enterprises, HJ Heinz, and Bloomberg are examples.

Private corporations are generally smaller than public corporations and often have less formal rules to follow. That's why a large public company will choose to go private. For example, in a *Wall Street Journal* commentary, Dell Computer founder Michael Dell observed, "Privatization has unleashed the passion of our team members who have the freedom to focus first on innovating for customers in a way that was not always possible when striving to meet the quarterly demands of Wall Street."

BOARD SEAT "SKILLS BUCKETS": WHAT ARE YOUR STRONG SUITS?

In researching what corporate boards want, I've identified two of what I call distinctive "skills buckets." One of these buckets will likely be a better fit for you over the other.

- "Always in Demand" Board Skills: These are the big-picture executive leadership skills that are universally in demand by most boards when they are seeking new directors.
- "Subject Matter" Board Skills: These are the skills from subject matter experts that boards pursue when such skills are mission critical to the company.

Let's take a look at each of these skills buckets in more detail.

1. ALWAYS IN DEMAND BOARD SKILLS

In a nutshell, corporate boards routinely seek very senior executives who have big-picture experience, possess keen operational and financial skills, and know firsthand how business works and the functions and processes that make it work.

"Always in Demand" titles include:

- CEO of a public company
- President of a large division of a public company
- CFO of a public company
- Board of directors experience with a large private company

  Note: Because there is a scarcity of CEOs, division presidents, and CFOs available for board service, corporate boards of directors are recruiting other C-suite titles. These titles are particularly attractive to boards when the candidate reports directly to the CEO or CFO. Examples include Chief Operations Officer, Chief Technology Officer, Chief Marketing Officer, and Chief Talent Officer.

"Always in Demand" corresponding experiences include:

- The ability to chair an audit committee
- The ability to sit on an audit committee
- The depth of knowledge to advise corporate boards on corporate governance (This is often the case for small-cap firms with limited legal resources internally.)
- The experience of setting executive compensation
- The ability of a CEO to help plan his/her own succession
- The mastery of profit and loss (P&L) financial statements (To be truly relevant, the person must thoroughly

understand revenue or sales targets, not just a cost center P&L. The candidate's revenue oversight is ideally three to five times the revenue of the company a candidate is hoping to serve as a board member.)

Note: If you're thinking "I don't have a C in my title, so I'm sunk," think again! Thousands of sitting board directors have executive suite backgrounds without a C title. But here's the caveat: As with the C-suite titles listed above, it's especially helpful if, in your executive suite position, you report (or have reported) directly to your corporation's CEO or, at a minimum, the CFO.

Two Types of Public Board Directors

In the case of public companies, a board is comprised of both "outside" and "inside" directors.

Outside director: An outside director, often referred to as an "independent director," is "independent" because they are not tethered to the company in any way. These directors are charged with remaining objective in monitoring a firm's management team and are responsible for holding management accountable for corporate actions that serve the best interests of the company. Corporate governance standards require public companies to have a certain number or percentage of outside directors. Above all, outside board directors are expected to look out for shareholders' interests.

Inside director: An inside director of a public company is a board member who is an employee, officer, or stakeholder in the company. Typical inside directors are:

- A chief executive officer (CEO) who may also be chairman of the board
- Other executives of the organization, such as its chief financial officer (CFO) or its executive vice president

Timing

The more recent your experience the more it is likely to appeal to boards. Some recruiters tell me that a CEO or a senior executive who's been retired for more than a year has less appeal to boards than do those currently employed or just retired. Because the world of business changes so quickly, it is essential that board members be up-to-date.

Let's look at this contemporary real-world example.

HomeAway, Inc. is a small-cap firm based in Austin, Texas, which was recently bought by travel giant Expedia.com. HomeAway is a leader in the online vacation rental marketplace, with more than 1,000,000 vacation rental listings in 190 countries. Seeking a new board member with extensive marketing experience in a closely "associated" industry, HomeAway recruited Southwest Airlines' Chief Marketing Officer, Kevin Krone.

As CMO, Kevin is responsible for Southwest's marketing strategies covering all sales and promotions; special event marketing; multicultural activities; partnership relationships; all field sales offices; advertising; Southwest's frequent flyer program called Rapid Rewards; online marketing; and distribution of Southwest's products. One particular skill that proved pivotal to Kevin's selection is his many years of leadership at Southwest aggressively expanding the airline's online customer service abilities. For HomeAway, social media plays a huge role in competing for the vacationer's rental dollar, and so they sought out a director like Kevin, who brought firsthand mastery of navigating the topsy-turvy world of social media.

2. SUBJECT MATTER BOARD SKILLS

If you are a professional with a deep subject matter specialty, your prospects for a corporate directorship may be rising rapidly! More than ever, today's boards are filling seats with highly specific "mission critical" skill sets. This is particularly true for small-cap firms where corporate resources are often more limited. Subject matter experts being seated at today's corporate board tables include those with command of:

Digital technology

Cyber fraud

Social media

International market entry

Employee engagement and retention

Corporate governance

Customer loyalty and retention

Scientific knowledge for science-based companies

Political navigation for heavily regulated companies

Want some really good news? The above list is just the tip of the iceberg. Given the rapid change in today's business world, new subject matter skills are constantly emerging.

FOUR DECISIONS TO SET YOUR BOARD SEAT STRATEGY

Making the following four decisions is crucial to setting your search strategy. As you weigh each decision (and in all of the preferences you name in this chapter), ask for what an advisor in a random article I read several years ago called AIR: advice, insight, and recommendations. Ask your friends and colleagues for AIR. Your awareness of your skills will likely be keener because of their help.

DECISION 1: CHOOSE THE SKILLS BUCKET THAT SUITS YOU BEST.

Pick one: Always in Demand or Subject Matter. State your reasons "why."

If you believe you have equally strong credentials in both buckets, by all means list them! The duality can give you a real advantage.

DECISION 2: DECLARE THE SKILLS THAT MAKE YOU MOST COMPETITIVE.

Within your chosen bucket, what particular skill set(s) do you consider most board worthy? Declare them! Be as specific as you can as you note what you have to offer to the board. This will help clarify your own mind and help if you involve a recruiter later on in finding the right board seat.

DECISION 3: PINPOINT THOSE INDUSTRIES YOU CAN BEST SERVE.

Within what industries do you believe corporate boards would find you most board worthy? To help you answer this question, consider these two different factors:

Career experience. Think about industries in which you have direct experience. That's likely where your board candidacy will be most appealing. But be careful here. If you are about to retire, for example, your employment agreement may include a non-compete clause. That provision could restrict you from serving on the board of a firm in direct competition with your current employer.

Adjacent industries. What adjacent industries serve the companies in which you have worked or have business challenges that are compatible with your own experience? Often, your best board seat opportunities reside in these adjacent industries.

Take a look at how one of my interviewees parlayed her experience into an adjacent industry.

Like many first-time directors, Lori Gobillot's invitation to join the board of Bristow Group, a mid-cap offshore helicopter transport company, came through adjacent industry synchronicity. After law school and a stint at the global law firm of Vinson & Elkins, Lori joined Continental Airlines, where she had P & L responsibility for the development, leasing, and management of the airline's real estate facilities worldwide. She was ultimately elected an officer of Continental. During that time, Lori interviewed for a senior management position at Bristow Group, but she decided to continue with Continental where she went on to lead the company's merger integration planning and ultimate merger with United.

The earlier job interview, however, served an important function. It put Lori and her skill set squarely on the radar screen of the Bristow Group's CEO. Soon after leaving Continental to launch her consulting firm, a board seat opened up at Bristow. Lori was invited to interview and was ultimately asked to join the board, which she accepted.

Here's an excerpt from Bristow's fiscal year 2015 proxy about Lori's role as a board member:

"Ms. Gobillot is an attorney by education with extensive management and legal experience within the aviation industry as well as experience in private practice representing a variety of clients. Her years of experience at a capital-intensive airline with a similar focus on safety, regulatory compliance, customer service, and employee satisfaction add a helpful perspective to our Board's deliberations. Her aviation background and legal knowledge allow her to contribute significantly as a member of the Compensation Committee and benefit our Board's decision-making process."

DECISION 4: DECIDE WHAT SIZE COMPANY WILL MOST PRIZE YOU.

As you'll recall from the introduction, each public company has a "capitalization size": that is, the market value of the company's outstanding shares of stock. The four cap sizes are large-cap (customarily greater than $10B); mid-cap ($2B to $10B); small-cap ($300 M to $2B); and micro-cap (less then $300M).

Let's dig a little deeper into what the boards of public companies in these four categories look for in director candidates.

Large-cap boards seek seasoned directors with years of large company governance experience, "very big picture" business know-how, political acumen . . . or some combination of those exposures. Exceptions, of course, are candidates with extremely high professional profiles and/or exceptionally close relationships with people in high places.

In *Claiming Your Place at the Boardroom Table: The Essential Handbook for Excellence in Governance and Effective Directorship*, authors Thomas Bakewell and James J. Darazsdi share the story of Mellody Hobson's first board director appointment to an iconic large-cap company. Here's how it happened.

> "I helped Bill Bradley when he ran for president in 2000," Hobson recalled. "I worked as hard on his campaign as I worked on my job every single day. Obviously, we were unsuccessful. But then one day, Bill calls and says, 'I'm on the board of Starbucks, and I'm taking you with me.' I never imagined that was possible. I'm like this pipsqueak in Chicago" (p 24).

As the authors point out, Hobson was deeply modest in her self-assessment. A Princeton graduate, she began as an intern with and rose to be president of Ariel, a firm managing $3 billion in assets. She made a name for herself within the Bradley campaign, and her outstanding work planted a seed in Bill Bradley's mind.

While Mellody's story is awe-inspiring, it's an exception to the rule. Most in-the-know board recruiters and sitting board directors would advise you to explore directorships on boards that are mid-cap and/or small-cap.

Someone who is looking to be a board member for the first time would do well to look at mid-cap companies. With the right skill sets, a first-time director would be a key candidate for a mid-cap company board seat. Lori Gobillot's story earlier in this chapter is an example.

The sheer number of small-cap and micro-cap companies weighs in the favor of anyone seeking a seat at the corporate board table. A 2014 Barrington Research study found nearly 50 percent of exchange-listed companies have market capitalizations of less than $300 million. Almost 35 percent are smaller than $100 million in market capitalization.

All of those statistics mean two things, one slightly disadvantageous and the other definitely advantageous:

(1) Given the thin capitalizations and pervasive risks that can face many small-cap and micro-cap public companies, their boards are often more "hands-on," providing constant oversight. As a result, directors can be called upon on very short notice.

(2) Because these small-cap and micro-cap corporations have limited resources, however, their boards are increasingly seeking directors with specific subject matter expertise. Bottom line: Board doors are opening for many aspirants who would never have been considered before.

ARE THESE STORIES SIMILAR TO YOURS?

What follows are two case studies of how real people worked through these four decisions to determine the board strategy that was best for them. See if you recognize yourself in one or both of them.

CASE ONE

"John" is retiring from a distinguished career of thirty-plus years leading the sales and marketing teams for makers of fast-moving consumer goods distributed through mass merchandisers, the last of which was a $50-billion public company.

Decision 1: Choose the skill-set bucket that suits you best.
Although John has skills that lean heavily toward Always in Demand, his Subject Matter skills should be noted as well.

Decision 2: Declare the skills that make you most competitive.
John's experience as a VP of sales draws on his ability to forge deep, trustworthy relationships with vendors and colleagues across his industry. Consequently, his list includes a mix of both types of board skills—Always in Demand and Subject Matter.

- Senior vice president of sales reporting directly to CEO of his division (Always in Demand)
- Deep sales, marketing, and general management experience (Always in Demand)
- Reputation as strategic change agent (Always in Demand)
- Consensus builder (Always in Demand)
- Exceptional industry connections—past chair of consumer health products association (Always in Demand)
- Builder of iconic over-the-counter brands (Subject Matter)

- Expert in building consumer brand loyalty (Subject Matter)

Decision 3: Pinpoint those industries you can best serve.
John is under a non-compete clause for two years, which limits his pursuit of board work with direct competitors. In the meantime, he can pursue adjacent industries. Examples include:

- Boards whose firms produce fast-moving consumer goods in mass merchandisers, including food and beverage and consumer electronics.
- Boards whose firms are service providers to consumer goods manufacturers. Examples could include packaging manufacturers and point-of-sale data suppliers.

Decision 4: Decide what size company will most prize you.
Given John's executive leadership experience, it appears that serving on the board for a public mid-cap firm ($2B to $10B in capitalization) would be his most prestigious director seat. While private and nonprofits are always worthy of pursuit, a publicly traded mid-cap board is the prize.

John's Board Search Target

John's Ta-da! strategy
- Decision 1: Always in Demand skills (primary); Subject Matter (secondary)
- Decision 2: Board seat concentration could focus on oversight of sales, marketing, and executive management
- Decision 3: Best adjacent industry sectors: (1) Fast-moving consumer goods in mass merchandisers, including food and beverage, consumer electronics; (2) Service providers to consumer goods

manufacturers. Examples could include packaging manufacturers and point-of-sale data suppliers.

- Decision 4:   Size—mid-cap firms

CASE TWO

"Jane," newly retired, has a proven track record that spans thirty-seven years of technical and business accomplishment in oil and gas, refining, chemical, and pharmaceutical companies. She has extensive leadership experience in all aspects of building and operating international manufacturing sites.

Decision 1: Choose the skills bucket that suits you best.

Jane reflects on her career and selects the Always in Demand skills bucket as the one that suits her best.

Decision 2: Declare the skills that make you most competitive.

Jane's board resume has a section of "firsts": first female project manager at a large oil company; first female construction manager; and first female manager sent overseas, among others. Her list of skills highlights the following core strengths:

- Business unit president of $1B unit with full P & L responsibility
- COO with oversight of global manufacturing and supply chain
- Formed and led operational integration of Fortune 100 merger
- Currently serves on the audit committee for a private company that provides management software for complex construction projects worldwide
- Noted thought-leader on operational and manufacturing leadership

Decision 3: Pinpoint those industries you can best serve.

Jane's non-compete clause is about to expire. She is well suited for boards whose firms manufacture such devices as pumps, valves, pipes, compressors, measurement tools, and other equipment related to the oil and gas industry.

Decision 4: Decide what size company will most prize you.

Jane's extensive experience in manufacturing, operations, and audits is in big demand. The one wrinkle in her resume is that she has not reported directly to a CEO. Because of the absence of that credential, I would recommend that Jane consider serving as a board director for a public small-cap firm ($300 M to $2B in capitalization). With more board experience, Jane is likely to attract mid-cap board seats soon.

Jane's Board Search Target

Jane's Ta-da! strategy

- Decision 1: Always in demand skills
- Decision 2: Board concentration could focus on oversight of manufacturing, operations, large complex internal construction projects
- Decision 3: Best adjacent industry sectors: firms that manufacture pumps, valves, pipes, compressors, measurement tools
- Decision 4: Size—small-cap firms

I can help you dramatically shorten your time and effort in pinpointing the "right" boards. Refer to BoardSearchAccelerator. com in the "Resources" section at the end of this book.

When the Fit Is Not So Apparent

A board recruiter posted a board query on a women's professional board director site and Melanie Barstad responded. The Cintas board was looking for a female candidate with public company CEO experience. Prior to retiring from Johnson & Johnson, Melanie had served at the executive level as a member of several J&J operating companies' management boards. While she had not held the CEO title, the fit was close, so she contacted the recruiter.

The recruiter was a bit doubtful, but she sent Melanie's credentials forward anyway. Melanie's instincts proved right. Several factors gave Melanie an advantage: Cintas was a family-owned business that went public and had big growth aspirations. Melanie had a long track record at J&J helping the former family-owned firm do exactly that. Cintas wanted to grow its healthcare industry uniform business. Melanie had extensive healthcare sector experience. After careful vetting by the board (and her careful vetting of Cintas in return), Melanie received and accepted Cintas's invitation to join the board.

"The lesson," says Melanie, "is that sometimes a board doesn't know what it needs until they see it." (More of Melanie's story continues in chapter 4.)

ESTABLISH YOUR BOARD-WORTHY SKILLS

Now that you've zeroed in on the size and type of board you'll target, knowing what strengths you'll offer them, the next step is to polish those skills. As my mom always said, "Rome wasn't built in a day." So be patient with yourself. Things will work out.

The sooner you begin preparing for a corporate directorship, the better. And to help you begin to prepare, here are some early actions to consider for the purpose of fine-tuning your skills.

Seek out for-profit private board experience. In an article for CBS News, Marie Baca shares important wisdom from Steve Mader, the managing director of board and CEO services for recruitment company Korn Ferry: "Although any board experience is beneficial, corporations are likely to value for-profit board experience over a directorship at a nonprofit." Find a small company or start-up and approach it about serving on its board. Be upfront with these firms about their stepping-stone appeal. And if five years is your limit, don't sign up for something that could last a decade, Mader advises. "You want to think short term, and you want to do that in good conscience."

Consider not-for-profit opportunities. To take the contrarian position to the above point, nonprofit boards can be a valuable launching pad for corporate board service. Perhaps the most worthy nonprofit credential is a seat with fiduciary responsibility. That means joining a board of trustees, for example, rather than an advisory board. Nonprofits, particularly large ones, allow you to work closely with high-ranking corporate and community leaders. In addition, landing a seat that enables you to closely support the nonprofit CEO on board governance matters can be very valuable.

Plan strategically for a corporate board seat. When Australian Anne Ward left twenty-five years of private practice as a commercial lawyer to move to a senior executive role in a major bank, she was making a conscious move toward a future public company board career. She had extensive board experience in the not-for-profit sector, particularly in statutory matters, which she gained while working in her full-time day job as a lawyer. But she took note when sitting public company directors advised her that it would be helpful for her to have senior executive experience when she looked for directorships on public boards. That sage advice paid off. She currently holds directorships at Australian corporations Zoos Victoria, Colonial First State, and Flexigroup Limited.

Continually sharpen your subject matter expertise. Board seat competition is fierce. You'll need to be perceived as one of the best in your skill-set niche. Involvement and presentation at your industry's annual conferences, deep self-study of industry advancements, combined with writing white papers, book chapters, or books as well as searching out industry leaders as mentors are a few of the ways to begin now to establish yourself as a true expert in your field.

Strive for the executive suite. Showing senior executive experience on your resume greatly raises your probability for a corporate board seat. The Houston Women's Chamber of Commerce and the Tri-Cities Chapter of the National Association of Corporate Directors recently sponsored a program for which I moderated a panel called "Charting My Course from the Executive Suite to the Board Seat." Each panelist's story had a common denominator: Years, even decades, of doing stellar work every day (and making sure they got credit for it), and a willingness to stretch and grow their management and leadership skills were critical to being tapped for the executive suite.

This sounds like a lot of work, doesn't it? But remember the famous words of team manager Jimmy Dugan (played superbly by Tom Hanks) in the popular movie *A League of Their Own*: "It's supposed to be hard. If it wasn't hard everyone would do it. It's the hard that makes it great."

Want to greatly reduce your time finding your ideal board seat? Visit BoardSearchAccelerator.com.

TOOLS FOR YOUR JOURNEY

- "What does a *board* want?" is the first question every board aspirant should ask.
- Boards seek out two skills buckets: Always in Demand big-picture leadership skills and Subject Matter expertise. Know your best buckets.
- Your best chances at winning a corporate board seat are arguably on small- and micro-cap public companies. These firms are ample in number. And because of their limited resources, they need specialized knowledge and are increasingly seeking board directors with skill sets that are new to their boardrooms.
- Use the four key decisions to drive your board search strategy.
- Often, your best board seat opportunities reside in adjacent industries that serve the companies in which you have worked.
- Ask for AIR: advice, insight, and recommendations. Your knowledgeable supporters can help you tweak your strategy.
- To get there early, start now to prepare for a corporate board directorship.

ACTION #3:

FINDING BOARDS THAT WOULD WELCOME YOU

*"Vision without action is a daydream. Action
without vision is a nightmare."*
—Japanese proverb

In the previous chapter, you made four decisions that ultimately netted you a strategic road map for choosing companies that could be good "pursuits" as you look to secure a corporate board seat.

Now it's time to put your newfound strategy to use to identify companies that are good matches for you and to begin to investigate them further.

ACTION BREEDS CLARITY

Here's what's so great about compiling your list at this stage: Action breeds clarity. The moment you start searching out companies for your list, you'll begin to assimilate information that will give you more and more insight as to where your best opportunities are (and are not). You'll have some "Holy cow!" moments that either send you in the opposite direction or make you want to dig deeper because you begin to see that a particular industry or firm could really be a great fit.

This is where we really start to add some meat to the bone.

COMPILE YOUR LIST

Look through the Fortune 1000 and Russell 3000 lists and compile a list of companies that appear to be the best fit for you. Organize the list using the strategic board search target information you identified in the previous chapter.

As you're compiling your list, be open-minded and focus on the quality of the opportunity. Try not to get hung up on the size of the company or the prestige of the brand name. Be realistic. At this point, you've probably already got some companies you are interested in.

VET YOUR LIST

Review annual reports, press releases, and analyst reports of each corporation you identified. Check out investor chat rooms and the blogosphere. If it's a company your colleagues know about, by all means get their input. During this investigative process, consider setting up Google alerts to keep abreast of current marketplace happenings for the firms on which you're focused. Often the juicy insight is found buried way down in the firm's search listings.

ELIMINATE POOR CONTENDERS

Consider those restrictions that would prohibit your service with the firms on your list. For example, ask yourself a range of questions such as these:

- Is the travel distance required to get to this firm's board meetings prohibitive?
- Do firms on my list represent a potential conflict of interest given my current business obligations?
- Are legal issues looming for this firm?
- Does the firm's product or service make me yawn? (Passion for the firm's mission is extremely important.)
- Does the current board membership seem a little too clubby? (Some clues to this could be that the members live in the same city, or they serve on a lot of the same boards.)

At this point, I'd like you to have a robust list of boards to prioritize and vet. I recommend you choose forty. Feel free to go higher or lower, of course; it's totally your call.

PRIORITIZE YOUR LIST

Now prioritize those firms that are your top picks. Zeroing in on the companies for which your experiences could be most useful will increase your chances of being considered.

Keep asking yourself: Can a strong case be made for why my skills make sense for this board?

Remember that prioritization is a good thing. Relentlessly zero in on the companies for which your experiences could be most useful. Resist the wild goose chase. Stay on the trail.

ASK FOR AIR: ADVICE, INSIGHT, AND RECOMMENDATIONS

You needed AIR in chapter 2 when mapping your strategy. Ask for AIR again here! Share your list with knowledgeable, trusted supporters to get their perspective and feedback. Consider their advice, and if it resonates, use it to add more viable contenders and to remove poor contenders.

"GRID" THE BOARDS THAT ARE YOUR TOP PRIORITY

You know I love grids. They help you connect the dots across categories of information. Consider these categories for your grid:

Company name

Industry

Meeting location

Board diversity

Years to board retirement

Current board members' areas of expertise

Directors who know you

The firm's general counsel

The firm's accounting firm

Other professional services that interact with the board

STAY FLEXIBLE

Always be open to amending your list. When new choices surface, look at them with an open mind. Most important, be flexible and listen to your instincts. It's been my experience that when you are clear about your intentions, the universe will align to help you.

TOOLS FOR YOUR JOURNEY

- Action breeds clarity. As you compile and vet a list of boards that might welcome you, you'll begin to see more clearly how marketable you are as a board director.

- Sift and winnow your long list of candidates—don't "hesitate to eliminate" (Ah, I love that alliteration!)—and prioritize the short list of strong contenders that are left standing.
- Make a grid with details about the boards on your Top 10 list. That way, you can quickly eyeball your information at a moment's notice.
- Remember that this is an ongoing process. Keep your list current. That way you're always ready for action should new possibilities appear on the horizon.

ACTION #4:
ATTRACTING BOARDS TO YOU

*"Your brand is what people say about you
when you're not in the room."*
—Jeff Bezos

How would a professional colleague describe you? Seasoned C-suite executive? Strategic pathfinder? Uncontested expert in your field?

That snap answer is your reputation, or in today's social media jargon, your "personal brand." As business guru and author Seth Godin explains in a blog post, "Your brand is a story, a set of emotions and expectations and a stand-in for how we think and feel about what you do" ("Logo vs. Brand," January 7, 2015).

Since board seats are by invitation only, it's critical that your personal brand attracts—or, more specifically, draws—the right boards to you. Here are some proven ways to make that happen.

YOUR PERSONAL BRAND

In interviewing sitting board directors for this book, I invariably asked each of them, "How did you get your first corporate board seat?" In tallying their answers, this common formula emerged:

Passionate Expertise + Fearless Work + Visibility + Recognition = Opportunity

Many directors identified their passions—that is, what energized them—early in their careers and what they were really, really good at doing. Then they persisted in fearlessly doing their work in visible places over many years, even decades. In time, they became branded by their skills and were recognized for their achievements.

Let's take a closer look at each of those four components.

PASSIONATE EXPERTISE

If you're reading this book you already know that finding what you love, and what loves you back, is the sure-fire way to ignite your drive to get really good at something. Board director Beryl Raff is a case in point. She is chairman and CEO of Helzberg Diamonds and serves or has served on the boards of directors for Helen of Troy, Automotive One, JCPenney, and Jo-Ann Fabric and Craft Stores.

> I had no career aspirations and am still shocked today that I have accomplished what I have. I was just a little Jewish girl from the Philly suburbs who thought she'd marry a doctor and have a family. I come from a retailing family, fell into what ultimately became Macy's training program, and I loved it—and poured myself into the work—and it loved me back.
>
> I did marry the doctor—two of them. And I did have a family, but not until I was almost thirty-nine.

FEARLESS WORK

Fearless work is what Libby Sartain brought to Southwest Airlines' executive committee in 1998. Libby now serves on the boards of directors for ManpowerGroup and AARP and has been a director for Peet's Coffee & Tea and SHRM Foundation. But in 1998, as head of the "People Department" (the airline's name for Human

Resources), Libby had just been given a seat on the committee. While conventional wisdom suggests executives new to such a high-powered committee hang back to learn the lay of the land, Libby demonstrated her fearless work ethic at the very first meeting. That's when she boldly proposed Southwest offer the same benefits to gay and lesbian employees that the company offered to employees in married and common-law relationships. Libby and her department viewed such benefits as health insurance as a significant portion of employee compensation; without them, gay and lesbian employees did not receive equal pay for their equal contributions. She shared the fact that 10 to 20 percent of the company's employees were gay or lesbian, and many were among the airline's "best" employees. (The first Fortune 500 company began offering same benefits to gay and lesbian employees in 1990.)

The committee turned down Libby's proposal, citing concern over higher "self-insured" costs. But Libby persisted. She consulted with Southwest President Colleen Barrett, who expressed support but looked to the executive committee to make the decision.

At the next meeting, Libby brought the proposal forward again. This time she proposed, and the committee agreed, that an "enlarged circle" of employees from across the company be formed to study the issue. What happened next is one for Southwest Airlines' history books. A breakthrough suggestion ensued from and was approved by the committee: Establish benefits for *all* employees with "committed partners." Proof of commitment included partners being named as beneficiary on each other's insurance policy and owning a home together or sharing rent.

Southwest joined the ranks of other Fortune 500 companies whose committed partners received equal pay for equal contribution.

It was a "fearless work" milestone for Libby and her department, and the attribute became part of Libby's personal brand.

Fearlessly Striving for the Board Seat

"Fearless work" also means stretching yourself through career moves that can make you more worthy to take your seat in a boardroom. I interviewed a woman board member who was in financial sales with a mutual fund company and explicitly asked to be moved to finance to learn the intricacies of balance sheets and income statements and all of the background data that preparing those documents involved. She eventually headed up the finance function at the mutual fund and she reported to the CEO. With that reporting credential in hand, she became a sought-out corporate board candidate and eventually joined several boards.

Another board director I interviewed served as president and CEO of a large investment management firm with more than $200 billion of assets under management. Her oversight included sales, product development, portfolio management, operations, finance, and technology. She reported to an independent board of directors. Before moving to that top position, she held senior vice president/controller positions in banking. She had purposely sought out the opportunity to move from a singular financial expertise as SVP to a top executive position. She saw the new position as the sure way to broaden her skill set and marketability. This broadening dramatically increased her attractiveness as a board candidate and was key to helping her earn her first public board seat.

VISIBILITY

Visibility is critical. You can do stellar work, but if it's not visible, it can't take you anywhere. Consider the following examples.

When Carole Brookins was CEO and chairwoman of World Perspectives Inc., a Washington-based consulting firm specializing in agricultural commodities, she gave a speech at a fertilizer-industry conference. After the keynote, the president of Terra Industries, a Sioux City–based fertilizer maker, approached her and a networking relationship began. A year later, when a board seat opened at his firm, he invited Brookins to interview. She landed the seat, her first of three corporate board director posts.

Lack of Visibility Can Cost You

Consider this short history lesson from the Al Ries and Jack Trout classic, *Positioning: The Battle for Your Mind* (McGraw-Hill Education, 2000).

> Christopher Columbus, who discovered America, was unrewarded for his efforts. His mistake was searching for gold and keeping quiet about his discovery.
>
> Enter Amerigo Vespucci, who was five years behind Columbus. He took a different approach. First, he positioned the New World totally apart from Asia, which caused a really big stir. Secondly, he wrote substantially of his theories and discoveries through letters, one of which was translated into forty languages over more than two decades. As a result, Europe accredited Vespucci with discovering America and named the continent after him.
>
> And Christopher Columbus? He died in jail.

For years, Linda Miller, Associate Professor in the Engineering Management Graduate Program at the University of Kansas, lectured to Midwest manufacturing executives on "Marketing for Manufacturing." Her expertise and visibility got her noticed by MGP Ingredients, a small-cap manufacturer of wheat- and corn-based ingredient technologies for the branded packaged-goods industry. She served on the board for fourteen years.

RECOGNITION

The old saying goes, "People buy differences, not similarities." But I know firsthand how unsettling (and downright scary) it can be to step out and make your differences known.

Here's My Story

In 1988, I launched a solo marketing practice in Austin, Texas. After years at R.J. Reynolds Tobacco Company as a brand manager and a short stint as director of marketing and sales for a start-up hotel company (eventually rebranded as Hyatt Place), I decided to start a boutique firm to help clients get and keep customers. Early awareness of my work was limited to the Austin marketplace, but I knew I wanted a national (if possible, international) presence. I studied the leaders in my field and saw one common denominator: Each had published a book with a reputable publisher. Bottom line: I needed to write a book.

At the time, the market was flooded with books on customer satisfaction and customer service. Every major publisher was already selling a number of such titles. To earn the right to publish, I would have to position my book as very different. That's when I dug deep into my experience and ultimately decided to write on customer loyalty—specifically, why firms should strive for customer loyalty, not merely customer satisfaction.

Going in this direction I felt unsure and apprehensive at every step. "Why isn't there already a book about customer loyalty?" I asked myself. "Am I going to be creamed by all the customer satisfaction and service gurus? If I'm professionally embarrassed, can I recover?"

I poured myself into research, scouring every source I could find to build a case for customer loyalty. I endured some big setbacks, even stopping altogether for several months, unsure of my way. But with the aid of generous people and some big helpings of serendipity, seven long years of toil paid off.

I delivered the manuscript. During the entire writing process, I lacked the confidence to ask even one colleague or friend to take a peek at it. I felt I would rather hear "It's bad" from an editor than from someone who really knew me. That's how scared and uncertain I was!

My editor liked the book. And with a few tweaks here and there, the manuscript was accepted.

Finally, in September 1995, my book *Customer Loyalty: How to Earn It, How to Keep It* was published by Lexington Books (a division of Simon & Schuster).

About the same time, noted business strategy expert Fred Reichheld, a Bain & Company Fellow, released *The Loyalty Effect* (published by Harvard University Press). Our books were often reviewed side by side. Reichheld's book, and the marketing reach of Bain Capital, raised the marketing awareness and importance of customer loyalty, and my book and my credibility rose with it.

The publication of *Customer Loyalty* gave me a presence on the national—and, ultimately, the international—stage for leadership in this emerging field. Suddenly, Fortune 500 corporations were calling *me* for keynote speeches and consulting work.

Several months after the book's release, I received an unexpected phone call from the renowned business entrepreneur and professional sports team owner Red McCombs, whom I had never had the pleasure of meeting. "I am in the car business," he modestly explained, "and I always knew we were missing something in our JD Powers customer satisfaction ratings, but I couldn't put my finger on it. Then I read the first chapter of your book and 'got it.' It's not just about building customer satisfaction, it's about building customer loyalty."

I stayed in touch with Mr. McCombs. In 2001, my publisher asked me to write the second edition of *Customer Loyalty*, and I began that process. (That same year my coauthored book, *Customer Winback,* was released.) I reached out to Mr. McCombs to write an endorsement of the new edition and to help connect me with the United Services Auto Association. (Mr. McCombs graciously did both.) I wanted to ask a top executive at USAA to write the foreword for the book since the company is legendary for its high customer and employee loyalty.

USAA's board chairman, General Robert Herres, retired, penned a marvelous foreword that focused on General George Washington and the loyalty of the Continental Army and the application of those principles in business today.

In our conversations, General Herres shared that he was also the chairman of Luby's Inc. (a small-cap, San Antonio–based restaurant chain). As luck would have it, an Ivy League marketing professor was retiring from the board and there was an acknowledged need for a new director with my skill set. With General Herres's sponsorship, the Luby's board invited me to join and I accepted.

More Ways to Get Recognized

Being recognized for your expertise is critical. Here's some sage advice from personal positioning expert Dorie Clark, adapted from her Time.com article, "4 Ways to Stand Out and Gain Positive Recognition at Work" (April 21, 2015).

> **Embrace the power of your difference.** Scientist Eric Schadt, thanks to his early training in math and computer science, was one of the first to leverage the power of Big Data in

biology. For years, many other biologists were skeptical of his ideas, but Schadt persevered, and now has more than two hundred peer-reviewed journal articles to his name on subjects as diverse as Alzheimer's and diabetes. When your background is different from others'—because of your age, your gender, your education, or your past career experiences—you see the world in different ways, and that can lead to breakthroughs. Schadt was a true pioneer and in today's world, technology underlies medical research and development.

Make your expertise undeniable. It can be hard to be recognized as an expert right out of the gate if you're a generalist. But if you start with a niche, you can quickly outmaneuver the competition and demonstrate a superior knowledge of a narrow subject. As I described above, this worked for me when I published my first book, *Customer Loyalty*. For over a decade the "customer" books had addressed customer satisfaction and customer service, and the field was crowded. I came to see that people were more likely to listen to you on a variety of related subjects once your expertise was undeniable in one specific niche.

Build your network. It's always helpful to have a strong network of respected professionals who know you, trust you, and believe in you. But when your background is unconventional in a given context—for instance, a millennial in a top corporate role, or a woman in a venture-capital firm—it becomes essential. Your network can give you the kind of frank feedback you need in order to navigate office politics and complex dynamics, and these people can serve as cheerleaders when others doubt you based on surface criteria. Making an effort to have lunch with one new person and reconnect with at least one colleague in your inner circle on a weekly basis can keep your network strong. (I share more on networking in chapter 5.)

Share your knowledge. One of the best ways to convince skeptics of your merits is to prove you know what you're doing.

When you share your knowledge publicly—giving speeches, writing blog posts, or curating a smart Twitter feed about your industry—you demonstrate your competence clearly because you allow others to see what's inside your head. An additional advantage is that when you start to build up a broader following, those closest to you, such as coworkers who may have been questioning your credentials, have to reevaluate their feelings when their own friends start to talk about you and your ideas.

TWO ESSENTIAL BRANDING TOOLS

Your board resume is perhaps the most critical branding tool in your arsenal. I was coaching my close friend, Lisa Webb, on her board resume. I asked, "What's your mission in the world?" She didn't hesitate. Lisa knew it cold: "To help my clients be the best 'individual contributors' they can be." She's applied this skill to sports psychology and in her executive coaching of CEOs of major organizations. That "mission statement" at the top of your board resume can help you stand out.

Here's how other board candidates designed their "stand out" resumes.

CRAFTING A RESUME TO HIGHLIGHT YOUR BOARD QUALIFICATIONS

Your resume is typically more detailed than a bio is, and a bio can be easily drafted from your resume. With that in mind, consider these guidelines as you craft a resume to underscore your qualifications for a board directorship.

Know your own board currency. When crafting your resume for the boardroom, it's important to understand and communicate the worth, merit, and desirability you bring to the board seat. These attributes play a major role in building your appeal as a board member.

Case in point: When Australian Anne Ward prepared her boardroom CV (a common branding tool in Australia), she carefully translated her executive skills and her legal knowledge to board skills. As she explained in a conversation with the Korn Ferry Institute, published in a report in 2014, those skills included her ability to think analytically, to amalgamate huge quantities of information, and to ferret out and focus on an issue's salient points. In addition, she emphasized the risk radar that she had developed as a lawyer or, put another way, her ability to "smell the smoke," as she phrased it. In Anne's case, her deep experience advising companies on acquisitions and mergers, capital raising, and floats were also relevant boardroom skills that she called out on her CV.

Go beyond your own self-assessment. You've done this before in the process, but it's worth doing again. Experienced directors and influencers can always add more value. Please keep reaching out. Find a few seasoned public board directors who are willing to ask you probing questions and help you identify your greatest strengths. Ideally, reach out to veteran directors who are particularly articulate; ask for their help in framing your personal and professional story in language that would appeal to members of corporate boards.

Going solo. For most of us, having a network to help get a seat is always the best way into the boardroom. But Julie Goonewardene is an exception. Having the aspiration but absolutely no contacts at the American Medical Association, she was elected a trustee. How? By sending her substantial resume and a letter. But what a letter! It addressed Julie's deep passion about driving medical advancement and her eagerness to serve the world in that capac-

> Think of a *tenor* as a tone. The **meaning** of the Latin word *tenere* was "to hold to a course."

ity. No hand-delivered resume, no sponsor, nothing! Julie Goonewardene "asked" and "received." When the CEO described why Julie was her choice for this prestigious board, she said the "tenor" of Julie's letter persuaded her.

Bottom line: Words matter.

Frame your accomplishments through the lens of results and change. Boards want directors who have "been there, done that." Whenever possible, credit your team when listing accomplishments. Boards are always glad to see proof of team player acuity.

Seek out an experienced resume writer. There's a host of good board resume writers out there, so be sure to ask for recommendations. Find several with a proven track record for crafting board director candidate resumes that get results. Contact them and see if there's rapport. It's like anyone you choose to work with; the fit needs to be right. When I searched "professional resume writers for board of directors," I found links to many qualified writers.

All of the big search firms that offer board recruitment services have websites on which you can post your resume. Your resume belongs there as well. And don't forget your LinkedIn profile. Include your board aspiration information in your profile. It's quite easy to post your board resume as a link. (I'm not a techie and even I can do it!)

Also, seek out organizations whose mission is to help you gain a board seat. (See the list in the resources at the end of this book.) But be careful. Some firms bogusly claim they can get you a seat, when all they really want is your money! Watch out for this type of claim in any mailings you get; many of my friends tell me they receive such notices.

Customize as appropriate. As you launch your board seat search, your resume should address a broad audience. But when you become aware that you are a candidate for a particular seat, take the initiative to revise the resume and speak directly to that board's specificity and their skill gaps you can address. Just as you have tailored your resume when applying for specific jobs, there will be slight variations when you present your story to different boards. Remember Melanie Barstad from chapter 2? Cintas was looking for a female candidate with public company CEO experience; Melanie had not held a CEO position, but she had served at the executive level as a member of the management boards of several J&J operating companies. She stressed her unique advantages: Cintas was a family-owned business that went public and had big growth aspirations; Melanie had a long track record at J&J helping the former family-owned firm do exactly that. Cintas wanted to grow its healthcare industry uniform business; Melanie had extensive healthcare sector experience with J&J. Customizing her resume with these specifics granted her interview privilege, which ultimately led to the board seat.

Note: You can find my boardroom resume in the book's resources section.

Compose Your Resume Prudently

Peter Lagomarsino and James Rowe, partners in the Mintz Group, provide research and investigative services to boards, corporate counsel, and their advisors. Here's their sage advice for aspiring directors from a 2014 *Directors & Boards* article:

Edit your social media profiles. Social and professional networking sites can be useful, but we caution you to keep potentially controversial opinions, grievances, and other content under wraps. Be very careful with your privacy settings, and periodically search for your own profiles on Google, under your name and handle, to assure that what's private is kept private. We have found many damaging indiscretions on social media even from the most pedigreed executives.

Double-check your resume [for accuracy]. . . . Any background check nowadays should shine a spotlight on any discrepancies, from the name and location of the university, to the degree type, major, and dates of attendance and graduation (did you graduate?). The same is true for any jobs or boards omitted from your resume.

YOUR ELEVATOR PITCH

The term "elevator pitch" reflects the idea that you should be able to winningly deliver your value proposition in the time span of an elevator ride, or approximately thirty seconds. People will only remember a few words. If the conversation inside the elevator in those few seconds is interesting and value adding, the conversation will likely continue after the elevator ride or at least end in an exchange of business cards, a LinkedIn invite, or an invitation to schedule a meeting.

Think carefully about what you want your elevator pitch to convey. For example, a fashion executive attending Carolyn Chin and Susan Stautberg's Onboard Boot Camp delivered a board-focused elevator pitch to convey that her licensing experience could help a firm forge new markets and build a brand. Look closely at the words she chose: "Forge," "new," and "build" are powerful future-focused descriptors that quickly telegraph board value.

Draft a few elevator pitches. Test them on board-savvy friends and colleagues. Revise. Test. Repeat. Bottom line, always be perfecting!

My elevator pitch goes like this: My area of expertise is customer loyalty. At this time in my career, I mostly apply my skills to corporate and nonprofit board work.

MORE BRANDING TOOLS

My father was the branch manager of the Duke Power office in our little town of Marshville, North Carolina. The "big boss" in Charlotte graciously approved a remodeling of the office and the result was clear glass windows and doors. My father instinctively knew that his front office and the staff who served in it represented the company's brand. It was more important than ever that he chose those front-liners with great care. He did just that! He handpicked Carolyn Horn and Mabel Traywick to stand behind the office counter and welcome customers as they came through the glass door to pay their electric bill. The appearance of these two Duke Power women instantly telegraphed "professionalism," "kindness," and "helpfulness." I adored them both. My favorite of their many wonderful attributes? They dressed beautifully.

LOOK THE PART

First impressions are made at lightning speed. Research shows that in the first seven seconds of a meeting, strangers are drawing conclusions about you, just as you are about them. Furthermore, research has consistently proven that nonverbal cues have over *four times* the impact on the impression you make than anything you say.

When you meet someone for the first time, the second that person sets eyes on you, his or her brain makes countless judgments: Do you have authority and status? Are you trustworthy? Likeable? Competent? Confident?

You can't prevent people from making instant decisions. (The human brain has been hardwired for this for survival purposes since prehistoric times.) But you *can* learn to make this impression-making work in your favor.

Let's look at these time-honored ways to make sure you boost your nonverbal scores when meeting board seat influencers. (Special thanks to Dr. Linda Henman; I adapted many of these tips from her "Positioning Yourself for Board Member Seats as a CMO" webinar.)

Clothes: When I consider appropriate dress, I always picture Steve Jobs in his black turtleneck. (Jobs sought out famous designer Issey Miyake to design it.) The turtleneck conveyed simple elegance—personal brand attributes that Jobs intentionally conveyed about himself and Apple. My Luby's board colleague Arthur Emerson conveys simple elegance another way. At a recent meeting, he wore a perfectly tailored black sports coat, black open-collared shirt, and an ivory ascot. What do you want to convey? Is your personal brand being conveyed by what you wear?

Ask yourself what others are likely to wear and make your choice accordingly. When in doubt, dress up, not down. Appropriate dress varies between countries and cultures. So, when you will be in an unfamiliar setting or country, prepare by paying particular attention to the host's traditions and norms.

Grooming: A good haircut for women and a good haircut and shave for men are essential. Women's makeup should be neat and natural. Above all, for both men and women, make sure your choices make you feel "the part."

Jewelry: Understated jewelry is always the best choice. Since board circles lean toward the conservative, men should think twice before wearing jewelry other than a good watch and wedding band.

Pen: Invest in a good pen. It truly sends a message. (No pun intended!)

Briefcase: The only real option here is authentic leather.

Car: If and when you can, drive something in keeping with what board directors and senior execs drive.

ACT THE PART

Take a look at this short list of do's and don'ts to help you present yourself as board worthy.

Turn off your mobile/cell phone. Few things telegraph "I don't value your time" more than a mobile phone that is "live." Silencing you cell phone is always a good practice when you enter a meeting, interview, or business lunch or dinner.

Smile. As the old adage goes, "Smile and the world smiles with you." A warm smile goes a long way to create a good first impression. It will put both you and the other person—or conference table full of directors—at ease. But don't go overboard with this; you can come off seeming insincere and a "lightweight" if a smile or grin is frozen on your face.

Make eye contact. When you look directly into someone's eyes, you transmit energy, interest, and openness. One sure way to strengthen your eye contact is to make a point of noticing the eye color of your new acquaintance. But there's more to know about eye contact. I have a dear friend who studied eye movement in her graduate work in psychology. She's coached me to notice how often a person looks down and/or left when speaking to me. In such cases, the person is likely telling an untruth. I took a neural linguistic programming course years ago, and the instructor taught the same principle. Just saying.

Shake hands. The handshake is a quick, effective way to build rapport. Make it firm, but not a knuckle breaker. Research has found that it takes an average of three hours of continuous interaction with someone else to develop the same level of rapport that you can get with a single handshake.

Stand up straight. Power and status are nonverbally communicated by height and space. Standing erect, pulling your shoulders back, and holding your head straight are all signals of confidence and competence. Go to YouTube to check out Amy Cuddy's TEDGlobal Talk, "Your body language shapes who you are" (June 2012). She had me standing straighter the moment I finished watching her presentation.

Lean in slightly. Leaning forward "telegraphs" you're interested and engaged. But be mindful and respectful of the other person's space. Staying about two feet away is a safe rule of thumb.

Practice good manners. Don't guess at what is appropriate etiquette; get the answers. You will be networking with people who were taught wonderful manners from early childhood. Find a good etiquette book. (For women, a favorite is *Emily Post's Etiquette* by Peggy Post and Anna Post. For men, a favorite is *The Art of Manliness* by Brett McKay and Kate McKay. Read and refer to them often.)

SPEAK AND WRITE THE PART

You are your brand! How you speak and write is key to your branding.

Communicate through storytelling versus abstraction. Telling your experience in a story helps you get your point across in a memorable way. In her instructive book *Dare: Straight Talk on Confidence, Courage, and Career for Women in Charge* (Jossey-Bass, 2013), Becky Blalock, former technology C-suite executive, aptly advises that your concepts "are almost always most persuasive when wrapped in a story . . . Relate anecdotes. Show the concept in action—where it happened and and how it played out" (p 70). I have a number of friends who are great storytellers. They have the gift for perfectly setting the scene, creating a dilemma, and then delivering an unexpected ending. I've studied their techniques. While you may not be a natural-born storyteller, Google "How to tell a story." Plenty of folks out there want to help you.

Control your speaking voice. Unlike men, women must be careful not to speak in a squeaky, high-pitched voice. (Nervousness can bring this on.) Men, generally speaking, have a larger vocal tract, which essentially gives the resultant voice a lower-sounding timbre. Regardless of gender, take care to speak intelligible words and at a pace that is comfortable for the "receiving" colleague. Facial cues can tell you if you're on track.

I have a distinctly Southern accent and have learned first-hand the power of voice and speech. Experience has taught me to refer to my accent early in a conversation with a new acquaintance. It typically brings a light moment and gets the "where-are-you-from?" question immediately out of the way.

Show intellectual acuity. There's no substitute for being well read. My National Association of Corporate Board Directors colleague Mel Cooper makes a point to routinely read the NACD association news publications and e-mails to stay abreast of board governance trends. He has found that such reading helps him contribute significant ideas and solutions in board discussions. The proof *is* in the pudding: His insights have been noted by his fellow board members who, in turn, have sponsored him on other boards.

Write coherently. Make no mistake about it: Your writing makes an impression. Grammar, punctuation, and spelling do matter in all of your written communication . . . and that includes e-mail and even text messages. (You'll find me passing along my mom's instructions on thank-you notes in chapter 6.)

If you are a challenged writer, then reach out to a freelance editor for help on big documents. Also, in this age of e-mailing and texting, know that the handwritten note still goes a long way in making a positive impression.

Read widely. In addition to reading newspapers, periodicals, and blog posts, I am an enthusiastic book reader. I find that reading business books, history volumes, and biographies provides me with additional perspectives that are often "fresh information" in conversation with business colleagues. One board colleague mentioned that she always reads the sports section so she can banter with the guys on her boards.

Next time you start to binge-watch a Netflix series, ask yourself: Will this give me the intellectual firepower I need for provocative conversation during board seat networking? If your answer is no, consider turning off the television and picking up a book. (Tip: It may help if you pretend your high school literature teacher is watching you.)

TOOLS FOR YOUR JOURNEY

- The proven formula for professional success is Passionate Expertise + Fearless Work + Visibility + Recognition = Opportunity.
- Your "board-worthy" resume and elevator speech are critical. Master them.
- In formulating your resume, frame your accomplishments through the "lens" of results and change.
- When you become a candidate for a seat, customize your resume to speak to the board's skill gaps.
- Strive to look, act, speak, and write the part. Study the style and habits of board directors you admire.

ACTION #5:

NETWORKING WITH BOARD DIRECTORS AND INFLUENCERS

*"You can make more friends in two months by becoming
interested in other people than you can in two years
by trying to get other people interested in you."*
—Dale Carnegie

Networking is more than a fleeting conversation. It's a series of interactions. These connections are vital to helping you search out board opportunities. Moreover, when companies hone in on one or two candidates, they'll do reference checks among people they know and trust. As a result, it's critical to continuously expand and enrich your network and get to know people who can vouch for you.

NETWORKING RULES

In researching this chapter, I reached out to two of the most generous and talented networkers on the planet: John Pincelli—my college roommate's spouse and ace real estate executive, and

Ralph Hasson—a dear friend and board chair. I've factored in a good deal of their wise counsel in the networking rules that follow.

RULE #1: MAKE NETWORKING FRIEND MAKING.

If you connect with new people for any outcome other than friendship, watch out! Your networking "mojo" will dry up fast, and here's why. If you are concentrating only on yourself, people can feel your lack of true interest in them and will often move away. We all want to talk with people who listen when we talk and indicate that they care about what we say. We've all spoken with people who clearly are just waiting until it is their turn to talk about themselves and have no interest in what we are saying. That style is your fastest way *not* to succeed at a networking event!

Instead, think of networking as an activity to help you make potential new friends, learning what they are about and discovering possible ways to support them. This "friendship frame" shifts your thinking to help mode. It naturally opens you up to others and lessens your networking anxiety. Suddenly, there's a higher purpose for your networking than just promoting yourself.

RULE #2: FISH WHERE THE FISH ARE.

Landing a board seat is both a numbers game and a contacts game. Network in organizations that have members who are corporate board directors and board seat influencers. (See a list of such organizations in the resources at the end of this book.)

But don't stop there! Let your bank, law, public accounting, and consulting firm contacts know of your interest in being on a board and the value you would bring. If you are involved in charities, nonprofit organizations, or cultural organizations, those can also be great sources of high-level contacts.

RULE #3: ADDRESS PEOPLE BY NAME.

For most people, hearing their name spoken is the sweetest thing they can hear. And so, for that reason, when you call someone by name, it carries a ton of weight.

You and I both know people who are great with remembering the names of people they meet. Lady Bird Johnson, former first lady and a shrewd businesswoman, was also famous for remembering people's names. A friend of mine tells the story of meeting Mrs. Johnson at a fairly large social event at the old Headliner's Club in Austin, Texas. He was not in politics, nor was he particularly influential. They had a short "nice-to-meet-you" chat and moved on. The next time he saw Lady Bird was twenty-five years later, at another large gathering. When he approached her to speak, she held out her hand and said, "Well hello, Bob, it is so good to see you again!" He was speechless. Lady Bird Johnson met thousands of people in her busy lifetime, but she made the effort to imprint names with faces when she met each one. It served her well in her own businesses and her husband in his political pursuits.

Research has convinced me that this talent for recalling a person's name can be mastered if we focus. So when you meet new acquaintances, focus on their names when they introduce themselves. You'll be surprised how far your concentration takes you!

RULE #4: TIT-FOR-TAT IS POOR FORM.

Give first. Then give again. And again. Do kindnesses for people because you can, not for what's in it for you down the road. Practicing tit-for-tat can poison the natural energy that rises from "best self" networking. Don't let it contaminate your intentions. Bottom line: Build your brand as a "go to" person who is always ready to help.

RULE #5: THINK FUNCTION, NOT JUST TITLE.

Next time you sit at an event table and find an administrative assistant seated next to you, REJOICE. This person knows how to make things happen. She (sometimes it's a he) knows processes and people within her company that her CEO is likely clueless about. Fate has likely dealt you a great card here. Make the connection, explore her interests, and if your instincts say so, nurture the unique new friendship.

RULE #6: ASK A BARBARA WALTERS WARM-UP QUESTION.

One of the best at the art of conversation is Barbara Walters. The depth and breadth of her interviews spanning five decades is legendary. A "get to know you" question she recommends is simply, "What was your first job?" Barbara says it's an easy question for anyone to answer, and the "Tell me more about that" follow-up query always brings interesting insights to the surface.

RULE #7: MAKE IT PERSONAL: "HOW'S YOUR MAMA?"

Imagine being "hit up" for business favors everywhere you go. Many senior business executives are faced with this daily: Someone is always wanting something from them. When meeting these execs, don't fall into this trap. Show an interest in a person's life, not just their work. Be the exception to the rule. You'll be a breath of fresh air.

A few years back, a Texas friend took the initiative to introduce me to her close colleague and friend—a highly successful professional in Columbia, South Carolina, who served on several prestigious boards and held the top national leadership position in his professional association. We arranged to meet at the tailgate he and his wife were hosting for a university football game. With my college roommate, Ann, in tow, I met this man. Ann had told me she knew this man by reputation and vaguely knew his family. To my delight, it was quickly established that Ann's mother and his mother had played bridge together many years ago but had been out of touch for a very long time. My new acquaintance loved this fact. (He told us that he called his mother several times a week and often struggled to find a common topic of interest.) Ann gave him her mother's number. Early the next morning, Ann's phone rang, and it was her mother reporting that my new acquaintance's mother had just called her. Ann's mother was delighted to be back in touch with her bridge-playing friend after so many years. And can you imagine the joy the son (my new acquaintance) got from helping his mother reconnect with her friend?

According to my Texas friend, I made a great first impression.

RULE #8: SAY "YES" THOUGHTFULLY, PERFORM FULLY.

If a contact asks you for a favor, think carefully before saying "yes." By saying yes, you are obligating your time and efforts to deliver. You may need to state some caveats on exactly what you can deliver. Remember, your word is your bond.

As you become better networked, opportunities will come your way for which you know you are not the best choice. Use these times to show your team player chops. Offer up names that are better fits and offer to make the connections. I practice this with my consulting colleagues. They always appreciate it and more than return the favor.

Your network is comprised of a lot of mini-networks among whom word travels fast and furious. Your good name and reputation are priceless. Every yes (and no) is a "handle with care" situation.

RULE #9: ASK CAUTIOUSLY.

When a need surfaces that requires a favor from a contact in your network, proceed with care.

Frame your ask in a way that honors your contact and his or her insight and advice. This is particularly important in asking for help on getting seated on a corporate board. The less tactful approach is to ask directly: "Do you know any corporate boards seeking new directors?" This approach feels harsh since it seems to put your contact directly on the spot.

A better tact is to take "the ask" in a different direction. Bring your research on board fit (covered in chapter 3) to the conversation. It shows you've done your research. Share which business sectors you believe are suitable and the possible boards in that sector that may prize your skill sets. Conclude with a soft close such as "This is the type of company I think I could add value to. Do you think I'm on the right track?"

After they offer their feedback, say: "Thank you for that insight. Please keep me in mind."

Now, if your contact offers to reach out on your behalf to a specific board, great! But by not asking directly, and instead asking for guidance and advice, you've gingerly planted the seed about your interest in board service. And you've allowed the individual to remain comfortable and shown that you value his or her advice.

RULE #10: MAKE PEACE WITH FORMER ADVERSARIES.

Research suggests that destructive business relationships are as bad for you as are destructive personal relationships. Work to mend bridges. In my experience, there are few people who don't respond to an effort to heal an altercation.

Remember, it's a small world out there . . . and what goes around comes around.

TOOLS FOR YOUR JOURNEY

- Think of networking as an activity for making new friends, learning what they are about, and discovering possible ways to support them.
- Landing a board seat is both a numbers game and a contacts game.
- Calling someone by name inclines that person to like you.
- Do kindnesses for people because you can, not for what's in it for you.
- When meeting someone at a networking event, think function not just title.
- "What was your first job?" warms up a conversation early.
- Show interest in a person's life, not just their work.
- Always frame your "ask" in a way that honors your contacts and their insight and advice.

ACTION #6:
ACING YOUR BOARD INTERVIEWS

"Before anything else, preparation is the key to success."
—Alexander Graham Bell

When you receive an invitation to interview for a seat on a corporate board, it's a significant milestone. It means you've made it to the candidate "short list" and the board wants to know more about you. You'll also want to know more about them, and I'll show you ways to prepare for the interview. But first things first. Ask yourself whether you even want to be interviewed. Some of the deeper research you'll do to prepare is not something to undertake unless you accept the invitation, because it could be time wasted.

This is where the rubber meets the road, so to speak. To ace these conversations, it's important that you bring your "director" persona to these interviews. That's far different from speaking in the capacity of your more familiar persona as a senior executive or subject matter expert. Instead, this conversation is an exchange about your abilities to work as a member of a team that oversees the workings of the corporation at its highest levels.

And remember to empower yourself with this knowledge: As the board members are evaluating you, you are vetting them too! This is a two-way street.

I've adapted many of the following points from an excellent report titled "The Path to the Boardroom," written by Kim Van Der Zon and Martha Josephson of Egon Zehnder International, Inc., a firm whose services include board search and board consulting.

I. BEFORE THE INTERVIEW

The board interview process is complicated and can be a bit murky. Here are some tips to help you perform at your very best.

Know the logistics. You may receive a preliminary phone call or be asked to pay a visit to gauge your interest. Next up will be face-to-face interviews. You'll likely be interviewed by one, two, or all three of the following: the nominating committee, the board chairman, and the corporation's CEO.

Do your homework. Research and then research some more. Try to find out what life would be like as a member of this board. Just as every business has a "corporate climate," boards, too, have customary ways in which they relate to each other, the company, and its management team. Try to find out what the "board climate" is. Learn all you can about current board members: Who are they? What have they done? And what specific skills does each one bring to the board? Look for "holes" in areas of expertise and how, in a director role, you could fill in the missing pieces.

To help you envision how many people I'm talking about in this context, according to the 2014 National Association of Public Company Governance Survey, these are the average board sizes:

Large cap	11 members
Mid cap	9 members
Small cap	8 members
Micro cap	8 members

For example, reach out to your network with these questions in mind: "What is the tone at the top? Is the CEO willing to use the board in a positive way, or does the CEO see the board as a necessary hindrance that needs to be worked around?" Getting an early "read" on this point is important. And you can look for more clues about this during your actual interviews.

Pick your references with great care. Calling references is one of the first things an interviewer will do. You should ask each person's permission to be listed as a reference. And tell them in detail why they will be called and what "talking points" you would like them to cover. Ideally, you want your references to meet three requirements: (1) They are highly respected top leaders in their fields; (2) They have deep corporate board experience; and (3) They can talk with specificity about your readiness to serve on a corporate board. If you have presented to boards or worked with board committees, the people you worked with can be excellent references.

Remember, this is *not* a job interview. Simply stated, this should not be an interview focused around your management skills. Instead, these interviews should be a conversation about the firm and your preparedness and readiness to mentor management and oversee the corporation's achievement of its strategic plans.

Read closely and thoroughly board-director-level publications, blogs, and websites to get informed on a broad range of topics surrounding corporate governance.

Go even deeper. You've been invited to interview. Who in your network helped? Reach out to these contacts for additional insight about this board and what its members are looking for in a new director.

To further prepare for the interview, be prepared to speak to these points beyond what you covered in your board-ready resume.

1. Prioritize your strengths in relationship to the particular board that is interviewing you. What is the biggest skill set you bring to this board seat? Financial acumen? Executive compensation? International market expansion? (Refer to the skills buckets analysis you completed in chapter 2.)

2. Tie your strengths to accomplishments.

3. Speak to the progress over your career of how you matured in the areas that are part of your board-level value proposition.

4. Throughout your career you have moved up the ladder. Describe this ascension. This should also include your nonprofit work.

Throughout your conversation, speak to experiences that demonstrate these traits:

- Ability to prioritize and zero in on the critical issues
- Integrity
- Good judgment
- Strategic thinking abilities coupled with pragmatic tactical ideas
- High performance standards
- Financial literacy

Don't paint yourself into a corner. Topics such as protection of shareholder value, top-management compensation setting, CEO succession, and risk enterprise management can be fraught with subtlety and controversy. Give serious thought as to how to frame your answers. Your goal is to converse deeply about these subjects while remaining diplomatic and free of being pegged as a proponent of one ideology over another. It's a tall order, but being offered a seat on the board could very well depend on getting this right. For practice, consider writing out answers to anticipated questions using the boardroom "tenor and tone" you've uncovered in your readings.

Always be prepared for a broad range of topics and expect the unexpected. An aspiring board member told me her first interview was very informal: It was over a cup of coffee in the firm's dining hall with the CEO and the board chair. The topic was politics, a tricky subject in any venue! But she was careful to keep her comments neutral. Ultimately, she got the invite to join the board, so she clearly maneuvered the interview well.

Carefully prepare to answer "Why?" There's a wrong way and a right way to answer the question "Why do you want to serve on this board?"

The *wrong way* is to reply with a statement that suggests your main motivation in seeking this board seat is because it will be good for you professionally. For example, answers such as "This is my next logical career move," or, "This gives me an opportunity to learn" or, "I can take what I learn and apply it at my company" give boards clear signals that you are interested in the seat for your own personal advancement. This is never a good idea. These rookie answers will hurt you.

Instead, answer the question "why" in the *right way*. This means your answer will have two parts: (1) You will speak to your unique skill sets and how your professional experience can add value to the board; and (2) You will share what makes you interested specifically in *this board*. Prepare your answers in advance with a keen eye on answering what intrigues you about the company, what specific challenges it faces that you could expertly address, and why you feel a passion to serve.

Expect deep vetting. Be prepared to sign a consent form that grants a background check on you. In today's Digital Age, the verification of your degrees and licenses is easier than ever. Even the slightest appearance of impropriety can be a deal breaker. Expect the company to look at your candidacy with the "trust, but verify" attitude. If, for example, you were the CFO of a company while it was under SEC investigation, be prepared to answer questions about that period.

Know that the vetting process is likely to be long. Kim Van Der Zon and Martha Josephson explain the challenge well: "Director searches take as long or longer as searches for top executives, with long stretches of time between steps. Don't become unnerved by the length of the process or assume that you've been rejected. Boards have their own cadences for adding directors and they often advance the process in a deliberate, iterative way."

That said, however, let me share from my own experience that the process of being interviewed and offered a board seat can also be brief. The CEO of Luby's interviewed me, and the chairman of Luby's board of directors called me soon thereafter to tell me I had been approved by the board to stand for shareholder election. A few weeks later we were scheduled to have our first board meeting, and I received the customary "board book" to review prior to that meeting. Afterward the sitting board members hosted a "get to know you" dinner for the new directors. In the weeks that followed, I reached out at times for mentoring from the chairman and the chair of each committee on which I served. You may experience a longer orientation through company seminars and the like, but there was no time for that in this situation. We went right to work because of all of the pressing matters surrounding board governance.

II. DURING THE INTERVIEW

"People buy differences, not similarities" is a time-tested marketing principle. The same holds true for the board interview. Sell your differences.

Make yourself a category of one. Few directors I know have prepared themselves to oversee a corporation from the boardroom better than Dr. Judith Craven. After earning a BS in biology and English from Bowling Green State University, she completed premedical requirements at Texas Southern University before earning an MD from Baylor College of Medicine and, later, an MA in public health from the University of Texas School of Public Health. Dr. Craven has also completed the Harvard University Program for Senior Managers in Government at the John F. Kennedy School of Government.

Two boards, Sysco (the food supplier giant) and Luby's, have benefited from Dr. Craven's unique viewpoints as both a medical doctor and a distinguished public health expert. She gained a distinctive understanding of the food service industry after serving as director of public health for the City of Houston from 1980 through 1983. Her responsibilities included the regulation of all food service establishments in the city, with an emphasis on food safety and food handling. Dr. Craven provides critical oversight as Luby's grows its "Culinary Division," serving food to select hospitals and other medical institutions in Texas.

Be forthcoming. A search committee appreciates when a candidate is forthcoming about a potential issue. Early disclosure can help you build early trust bonds with the committee. If you have a "skeleton in your closet," consider disclosing it early in the interview before being asked about it. For example, an old DUI is likely to be revealed in your background check unless you have taken steps to have it sealed.

Use storytelling. Describing your skills and work style in the context of compelling stories and examples is always a good idea. The human mind is wired for story and retains the information better in that context. Inject these stories and examples with self-effacing humor and you've increased your likability factor. Always be careful not to come off as bragging or playing the superhero. Look for ways to recognize your staff and team members. The truth is, no one succeeds alone.

Stay calm and cool. Never take any question personally. In my career, I've had interviewers hit me with a "stress" question or two. Often, it was for the purpose of testing my temperament for a demanding role. Don't take the bait. Instead, stay loose, breathe, and when appropriate, inject some humor.

Refrain from cheerleading. Even though you may be a huge admirer of the company, speaking extravagantly and lavishly about the firm can come off as naive and patronizing. "I admire your company's accomplishments" is an example of conveying high regard without being gushy.

Show you are no stranger to the boardroom. If you've been a member of senior management, you likely have made presentations to your company's board many times. Those experiences have probably provided you with governance insights that could serve you well in your board interviewing process. Before the interviews, spend some time recalling your experiences presenting to your board(s) and what those experiences taught you. Then, think strategically as to whether these impressions are significant enough to be interwoven into the interview process. If so, it could give you an edge over other first-time candidates.

Ask YOUR questions. The interview is your opportunity to explore whether this board is the right "fit" for you. It also telegraphs your insightfulness.

Consider asking a number of the questions listed below. Note that I adapted some of them from "Tips for Would-be Directors" in the June 2015 issue of Spencer Stuart's "Becoming a Better Leader" online publication.

- What is the company's track record for creating value? This is particularly important if the CEO is a newcomer.

- How is board independence defined? Who are the independent directors and what are their backgrounds?

- What is the board's appetite for risk?

- How do behaviors and interpersonal relationships shape the quality of discussion and decision making?

- How does the board strike the balance between advice and control?

- How would you rate the board's collegiality?

- How are differences resolved?

- What are the board's charter and mission statement?

- What are the company's corporate governance processes, including defined roles and responsibilities and directors' decision boundaries?

- How proactive is the board in providing director orientation and training?

- Describe the board's performance evaluation process.

- How much time should I be prepared to contribute, and please describe the expected workload?

- How many committees does the board have and what are the committee names?

- What are the duties of the chair of the committee and what are the duties of the committee members?

- Is there an executive committee? If so, who serves on it and how does it shape other board discussions and decisions?

- Please tell me about the D&O (deletions and omissions) coverage.

- How are directors compensated?

- Please tell me about the company's major shareholders. How long have they held their stake in the company?

- Please tell me about your board's current ability to deal with key governance topics such as CEO and board succession, company strategy, culture, risk, and stakeholder relationships.

- Shareholder activism seems rampant these days. What's the company's history and where is it most vulnerable?

- Many public corporations are going private. Dell is one recent example. What's your opinion about this firm going private?

- As a board member, what keeps you up at night?

III. AFTER THE INTERVIEW

Congratulations! You made it through the interview process. Now "put the cherry on top of the sundae" with these final steps.

Send a note of gratitude. That same day, write a handwritten note of thanks to each person who interviewed you and get it in the mail. (My Southern-raised mother is nodding "yes" from above!) And no, an e-mail will not suffice!

Seek out feedback from both the board and your sponsors. This is an important, helpful step not only after the interview process but also even if you are *not* chosen for the seat. When we look at feedback as a great way to point us toward getting better, and we apply what we can learn from it, a magical thing happens: We actually do become better.

I interviewed an aspiring board director who came very close to getting a seat. The board had two openings. A new CEO had been recruited and all of the existing board members had very close ties with the former CEO, now chairman of the board. The process went on for five months and my contact was told informally she had the seat. Then the tide suddenly turned. The board elected to fill just one board seat with a candidate who came highly recommended by the chairman. The second board seat was left unfilled.

There are at least three lessons here: First, even when you're told the seat is yours, it does not always work out. Second, sponsorship is key. The candidate who got the nod was endorsed by the chairman of the board. Chances are, if the woman I interviewed had had a top-level inside advocate she could have been invited as well. Third, asked to be reconsidered when another seat vacates.

Lesson: It matters who you know.

TOOLS FOR YOUR JOURNEY

- Hands down, the biggest thing the board will judge you on is "fit." Do they like you? Can they trust you? Can they work with you? Everything else is secondary.
- Remind yourself: You are being interviewed, but this is a two-way street. They must pass "muster" with you as well.
- The "why do you want to serve?" question is key. Focus on what intrigues you about the company, what specific challenges it faces that you could expertly address, and why you feel a passion to serve. Rehearse.
- Write that hand-written thank-you note! (I may haunt you if you don't.)
- Didn't get the invite? Get the skinny on why. It's your most valuable insight to improve your probability next go-round.

ACTION #7:
VETTING YOUR BOARD INVITATIONS

*"Take nothing on its looks; take everything
on evidence. There's no better rule."*
—Charles Dickens

Your decision to accept a board position is a big one. It's always useful to weigh the pros and cons again before you accept or decline the invitation. You'll be familiar with some of the guidelines listed below because of the research you did earlier on in selecting your "best fit" companies and in preparing for your interview. It won't hurt to put them into practice once again as you make your critical decision about joining a corporate board.

1. DON'T FIGHT YOUR CALENDAR.
As with life itself, sometimes it's the simplest thing that can complicate saying yes to a board invitation. In this case, it may be your calendar.

Board meeting attendance is important. So important that it is reported on in the corporation's proxy. A typical statement may read, "Each director attended 90 percent/all of the meetings of the board and committee(s) on which he or she served."

When comparing both your business and personal calendars against the board's meeting schedule, be sure to also take into account the travel time required to and from the board meetings. One sitting CFO I interviewed who had agreed to accept a board seat did so because the meetings were in Dallas and she lived and worked in Austin. Any more distance, she told me, and the time away from her current responsibilities was too prohibitive.

2. CAN YOU TRUST THESE PEOPLE?

As in anything in life, it's all about trust.

So, just how do you determine trust-ability? Think: R-E-S-P-E-C-T.

Ask yourself these questions:

- Is the company held in high regard?
- Is the board respected?
- What are the reputations of the board's individual members? While the reputation of each and every board member matters, pay particular attention to the chairman of the board's. This person's character must be beyond reproach. I have been blessed to serve with two such chairmen: the late General Robert Herres, and Gasper Muir, our current Luby's board chair. Both men courageously led our board through a number of crises and steered us to safe waters.
- Who else may be joining the board when you do? What are the backgrounds and reputations of those new directors?

Beware: Your reputation can be damaged by associating with a company that appears to be failing or is deeply involved in a major controversy. Perhaps Theodore Dysart, managing partner for Heidrick & Struggles' Global Board of Directors Practice, put it best: "It gets down to one thing: If this board blows up like an Enron, will I want to be in a foxhole with these folks?" (Dysart was quoted in a 2006 article in BusinessWeek by Toddi Gutner.)

At this point in your journey to the boardroom, you likely have a broad network of board directors and board influencers that can help you vet a board invitation. Reach out!

3. IS THERE TOO MUCH CLUBBINESS?

One board director aspirant I interviewed told me of a board that approached her about a potential vacancy. Each director of the all-male board lived in the same city. (She lived in a different city.) Many belonged to the same club, and one board member had served since 1949! She felt their invitation was all about appearances, and the main reason they sought her out was because of her gender. Wanting to serve where she could have an impact—not simply help a board appear to be nonsexist—she recognized these factors as big red flags. She passed.

4. RESEARCH, THEN RESEARCH SOME MORE.

Even if you interact with a broad network of experienced people, you may sometimes need more information, and it is your job to find out as much as you can before you commit to board membership. Use online search to vet the company and every board director. Although, as we all know, everything you read on the Internet is not necessarily true, what you learn may point to issues you will want to address. Do your homework.

Look Before You Leap

Exiting a board before your term ends is difficult at best, and it can jeopardize your chances for another board invitation. Consequently, when you say yes, be confident that you can fill out the term.

5. DO YOU FEEL THE PASSION?

Do you feel passion for the firm's mission?

We all know passion makes "work" feel like play. So, ask yourself this question: "Do I have a natural interest and affinity for the firm's products and services?" If your answer is no, think carefully before you say yes.

One of the board directors I interviewed turned down a board seat with a technology company that manufactured business-to-business (B2B) servers and routers because she didn't feel the passion for the product. She preferred tangible consumer products that she understood and, in turn, could go into stores to see and touch. If you find that you will decline an invitation to join a board, it's still a perfect opportunity to recommend a deserving colleague. Never pass up that opportunity!

6. EVALUATE RISK THROUGH "INSIDER" INTERVIEWS.

A corporation's "risk factors" are typically described in the corporation's 10-K report, so that's essential reading as you deliberate over your decision about the invitation to join a board. But consider digging even deeper by tapping two key sources: the company's general counsel and the independent auditor's lead partner. Of course, they will not share propriety information, but it's a good practice to seek out their expertise on what risks the company faces both externally and internally. My preference in these circumstances is to schedule a face-to-face meeting.

7. RESEARCH LAWSUITS.

All corporations have pending lawsuits. It's the world we live in. You'll find some mention on lawsuits in 10-K and 10-Q reports. Read them knowing that firms practice "less is more" in those disclosures.

It's always a good idea to dig deep. For example, do searches combining the company name with such words such as "fraud" and "derivative action."

Likewise, do a search on each sitting director. Always wade deep into the listings. That's often where the "good stuff" is found.

Of course, it's common sense that a lawsuit filed against the board's directors is a big red flag. But to be certain, ask for a written representation from the firm that no lawsuits are pending against the board.

8. INVESTIGATE DIRECTOR INSURANCE.

Make sure you're adequately protected! Review coverage levels with an outside risk manager. If you're not satisfied, request that the company consider buying an additional policy to cover independent director liability. If they are unwilling to add more director insurance (and you've uncovered considerable risk), this may be a deal breaker.

9. STAY OPEN-MINDED.

One of the best ways to show you what I mean about open-mindedness is to tell you my story about accepting a seat on a corporate board.

When I said yes to the Luby's board invitation, the company was $120 million in default with their banks. (Say *what?*) Here's how my favorable decision unfolded.

I consulted a seasoned transactional attorney who was very knowledgeable on corporate risk and directors and officers liability insurance. She advised me not to take the seat. But another advisor had a different perspective. He felt the "risk" period was closing. His rationale was two pronged: First, the banks were not closing in on the default. Luby's owned much of the property its restaurants sat on, so the banks were being patient. Second, the year before, highly regarded restaurant operators Chris and Harris Pappas had infused major capital, joined the board, and become the company's CEO and COO, respectively. In addition, two well-regarded veteran public board directors were joining the board as I was joining. I took the risk, and took the seat, and am so pleased I did.

10. TILL NEXT TIME
When you decline an invitation, do it with grace. Thank the board for the invitation, give a clue as to why you are declining, and if it feels right, you might want to advise them you would reconsider at some time in the future. Never burn a bridge.

TOOLS FOR YOUR JOURNEY

- It may simply be your calendar that precludes you from accepting a board seat invitation.
- If your instincts say you can't trust the people on the board, don't sign up.
- Lack of trust wears many masks. The more you get frustrated with the board on which you serve, the less productive you will be. Lack of productivity sends a huge ripple effect across the board and senior

management, and it can affect the firm's bottom line. Look carefully at trust and fit. Without these, your experience is bound to be a negative one, and it can affect your reputation.

- Feeling passionate about the firm's mission and its offerings is important. It's a guarantee you won't be bored.
- Research. Research. Research.
- Get an expert to review the insurance coverage you are provided as a director.
- Be open-minded. If current financial circumstances are bleak, step back and consider the big picture. That may be the perfect time to join! As the old saying goes, "It's always darkest before the dawn."
- Never burn a bridge.

CONNECTING WOMAN-TO-WOMAN: A SPECIAL MESSAGE

"A woman's natural aptitude for intuition, diplomacy, and value-based decision making are critical to leadership."
—Dr. Judith Craven

Women on Corporate Boards

As we saw in the *Harvard Business Review* article I cited in the introduction, women make teams smarter. Yet, although progress is being made to seat more women on corporate boards, the newest research shows the seating is painfully slow. Corporations and even new businesses and start-ups have much work to do to bring more women on boards.

But first, let's look at the good news.

The Good News

- 70% of S&P 500 Boards report having at least one female director.[a]
- Women hold 19.2% of S&P 500 board seats, an up-tick from 16.9% in 2013.[b]
- This is significant because the 16.9% held steady for eight straight years.[c]

- 30 percent of new directors are female—an all-time high. Of the new women directors, 37 percent are subsidiary presidents or line/functional leaders.[b]
- Women gained 75 corporate board seats in 2015, compared to 52 seats in that same sector of companies in 2014.[d]
- 45 percent of all corporate boards now have 20 percent or greater women on their boards.[d]
- Companies in five sectors now have over 20 percent female board members. These sectors include consumer foods, beverages, household and personal products, packaging, and tobacco as well as financial services, health care, real estate, and utilities.[d]
- Female CEOs are making room for female directors. (See Joann E. Lublin's *Wall Street Journal* article listed in the resources.)

But now, let's look at the bad news.

The Bad News

- Women hold only 19 percent of S&P board seats of the 2015 Fortune 1000 US corporations. While the 2014 Fortune 1000 list was not included in the 2015 report, in 2014 the percentage of board seats held by women was a mere 16.9 of the 971 active companies.****
- Smaller/new companies are less diverse than are established companies. Of the 2015 Fortune 1000, 199 companies have joined since 2010. Of these, the percentage of board seats held by women is only 13.5 percent.****
- Over 55 percent of the companies that became inactive in the 2015 Women on Boards Gender Diversity Index were in the "Token" or "Zero" company categories. Of the newly inactive companies, nine were Token and seven were Zero.

The survey reports a clear correlation between fewer women directors and failure to maintain a presence on the index. (The Women on Boards Gender Diversity Index does not speak to causality.)[d]

[a]2014 NACD Public Company Governance Survey
[b]Spencer Stuart U.S. Board Index 2014
[c]2015 census by nonprofit group Catalyst
[d]2020 Women on Boards Gender Diversity Index: 2011–2015 Progress of Women Corporate Directors by Company Size, State and Sector.

As a woman, I feel deep empathy for any woman interested in serving on a corporate board. It is an experience I enjoy and want you to share.

For women, the board seat pursuit often requires some special self-awareness about being a leader. An often-overlooked challenge is the fragile process many women face in coming to see themselves as leaders. This can be true whether you, as a woman, are on a corporate leadership track or perhaps striving to be a subject matter leader in your field.

WOMEN MAKE GREAT LEADERS

"Becoming a leader involves much more than being put in a leadership role, acquiring new skills and adapting one's style to the requirements of that role. It involves a fundamental identity shift," reports Herminia Ibarra, Robin J. Ely, and Deborah Kolb in their *Harvard Business Review* article, "Women Rising: The Unseen Barriers" (September 2013).

What follows are eight principles to help you form and strengthen your "leadership muscle." (These suggestions work equally well for men, but because women may be less accustomed to following these principles, I've reserved them for this chapter addressed specifically to female readers.)

PRINCIPLE #1: EMBRACE YOUR SPECIAL GIFTS.

Research studies show time and again that a woman's brain is wired for emotional intelligence. This wiring makes us especially good at diplomacy, showing empathy, and finding the middle ground. Our intuition helps us be creative problem solvers. These are all prized leadership skills. Give them a prominent place in your tool kit.

For example, I have coached an EVP of Human Resources that started her career in the call center of her well-respected clothing catalog firm. She learned firsthand the nuances of customer needs and all of the frustrations a front-liner fielding endless calls can experience. This empathy and diplomacy make her a great board candidate.

Lesson: Apply every ounce of your intuition, empathy, and diplomacy when leading your troops. More than anything else, it is your ticket to the top.

PRINCIPLE #2: DON'T WAIT FOR PERMISSION.

People become leaders by internalizing a leadership identity and taking purposeful action. Here's how it happened for me.

In 1979, with a freshly minted MBA from the University of South Carolina, I was fortunate to be offered a number of jobs and chose to join RJR Tobacco Company's brand management department. (You may be thinking, "Tobacco? Jill, where was your conscience?" In my humble defense, I was born and raised in North Carolina. My great-grandparents were tobacco farmers. and I was taught as a kid to have "pride in tobacco.")

I loved the six years I invested with this company. I felt valued and my hard work was rewarded. I rose quickly from marketing assistant, to assistant brand manager, to brand manager. At the time of my promotion to brand manager, the available slot was the chewing tobacco brand RJ Gold. (I smile as I write this. No, I never sampled the product!) This brand was part of a group of specialty tobacco brands that were managed independently of RJR's iconic cigarette brands. But I knew I had nabbed a hard-to-come-by brand manager slot and was thrilled to have it. I reported to a very "traditional" group brand director who brought his decidedly paternal "keep her safe" perspective to his role as my supervisor.

The brand manager who preceded me was an experienced and passionate fisherman. His love for the sport (and the brand's chewing tobacco buyer demographics) had led him to contract with a producer who specialized in creating "branded" television fishing shows. The filming was to take place in interior Mexico, in a secluded bass fishing camp renowned for its "catch with every cast." Major-league baseball player Keith Hernandez was the guest celebrity fisherman.

The filming was scheduled for a couple of months after I assumed my new management duties. My predecessor had all of the details of the trip worked out, so I simply adopted his travel schedule. After all, I reasoned, I was now entrusted with major oversight duties for the RJ Gold brand, and therefore this filming. If my predecessor had planned to go on location, so should I. I suspected my manager would be reluctant to send me, so I purposely waited until late in the workweek to advise him of my Sunday departure. He was stunned. To his credit, he did not forbid me to go. But I could tell he was very uneasy.

I took the trip and the filming went well. My oversight on location proved valuable. A number of issues came up on set that only a seasoned brand representative could have guided. The show was shown on ESPN and received good ratings.

Fast-forward to my first day back at the office. A memo was released from the C-suite's executive vice president of brand marketing. It announced that, going forward, all international travel would require prior written approval from the EVP. I read the memo and instantly realized that "my" trip had triggered this memo. (This new policy could have prevented my trip from happening.) Its circulation sent the department grapevine into high gear. Colleagues told me much of the talk centered on how I took ownership of the project. No doubt, it helped me stand out. I ultimately was promoted to lead the corporation's largest brand, Winston.

Lesson: To lead, we as women must push ourselves out of our comfort zones and not wait for permission. It can feel uncomfortable to "take" leadership. Feel the fear, then step up and lead anyway.

PRINCIPLE #3: SYNCHRONIZE YOUR VISION AND VALUES TO DRIVE CHANGE.

Like all human beings, we have core values. These values influence our feelings and drive our priorities. But not all core values are created with full consciousness, so it's important to invest the time and energy required to get clarity on your values. This conscious identification helps ensure that your values are *yours*, not simply soaked up from what's surrounding you.

Research shows that one of the competencies for senior leadership is the ability to create a vision for change. The "how" around accomplishing that vision will be almost exclusively driven by your own value system. The clearer you are about your values, and the more you lead with them, the better. That clarity will empower you and prevent you from making decisions and choices "that don't quite feel right." Consider this case in point.

In *Dare* (which I called to your attention in chapter 4), Becky Blalock writes of Carol B. Tome who served as CFO of Home Depot during America's worst recession since the Great Depression. From 2006 to 2009 the company was hemorrhaging money, losing a total of $13 billion in sales during that catastrophic period. Carol was asked to analyze the situation and take action on store closings and business line exits as well as to reduce support staff by 10 percent.

The result? Under Carol's value-driven leadership, Home Depot met its revised financial targets a whopping full year ahead of goal, earning more than $70 billion in 2012, staving off huge layoffs, and keeping 331,000 people employed.

Carol describes the philosophies that drove those results.

> "All of our decisions as a leadership team were guided by our company's core values which stress taking care of associates, customers, communities and shareholders," says Carol. "When you stay focused on your core values, the decision-making process is straightforward. Because of this I never lost sight of my responsibility to these key groups, especially our associates. I realized that they were all counting on me, and that I couldn't let them down." . . .
>
> "For instance, when we decided to close our Expo [Design Center] business, I visited the impacted stores and talked to both customers and associates about our decision. . . . I wanted them to know that these were hard decisions that were not made lightly, and I wanted to shake their hands and personally thank associates for their service and customers for their business.
>
> "While we had to make difficult decisions, we also had ample opportunity to show that we were committed to taking

care of our store associates. While other companies were cutting bonuses and eliminating 401(K) matches, we chose to continue those incentives for our associates, as well as annual pay increases. The Home Depot's founders, Bernie Marcus and Arthur Blank, said that if you take care of the associates, they will take care of the customers and everything else takes care of itself. I believe in that philosophy to my core . . . and our investment has paid off. (pp 22-23)

Lesson: Consciously define your values. That clarity will empower you to lead with courage to make things happen.

PRINCIPLE #4: SPEAK UP

"We [as women sometimes] believe we should wait until we are absolutely sure that we are ready for something before we ask for it," says Valerie Jarrett, long-time advisor to Barrack Obama when he was senator and now as president. As told in the book *The Confidence Code*, by Katty Kay and Claire Shipman (HarperBusiness, 2014), her first lesson on speaking up went like this:

After a decade of hard work, Jarrett was told by a client that she was doing the work of her then-supervisor, explaining: "You need to be the boss. You need a promotion."

Says Jarrett, "I thought she was crazy, but she kept nudging me, for months and months and months." Finally, Jarrett took the plunge, and she remembers the experience of talking to her supervisor like it was yesterday. "I was so nervous, but I told him all of the reasons why I deserved it, and he, very quickly, just said, 'OK.'"

Many years later Jarrett quizzed her former boss, now a close friend, about why he didn't voluntarily offer her the promotion. He'd been busy, he said, and hadn't thought of it. Jarrett describes the female fallacy this way: "We all assume there's a reason why. We think, 'I'm not deserving, if I were, he'd recognize my talent. It's not up to me to point it out.'"

My Story

I learned the importance of "speaking up" the summer after I graduated with my bachelor's degree from the University of South Carolina. I desperately wanted to get my MBA but had no funds. I had been accepted into the program, but my request for financial aid went unanswered. Finally, midsummer, waitressing at the coast, I became desperate for an answer. I drove my beat-up three-speed Chevy Vega (which backfired at every gear change) to the university and made a quick stop at the Registrar's Office for a copy of my transcript. (I had stellar grades.) With evidence in hand, I camped outside the door of the MBA director's office until he could see me. Inside his office, I laid my transcript before him and made my case. He granted me a one-semester trial work fellowship. Renewal was based on grade performance. That determination to ask for what I needed set me on a trajectory to finish the two-year MBA program owing only $750.

Lesson: Don't wait to be recognized. Instead, speak up for what you want and need.

PRINCIPLE #5: LEVERAGE MEETING TIME.

How you leverage meetings can be key to being noticed and, ultimately, getting fast-tracked. In doing research for their book *Break Your Own Rules: How to Change the Patterns of Thinking That Block Women's Paths to Power* (Jossey-Bass, 2011), authors Jill Flynn, Kathryn Heath, and Mary Davis Holt noted that men tend to arrive early for meetings to get their choice of seats and to chat with colleagues. Participating in these informal advance conversations can help clarify the true purpose of a meeting, making it much easier to take an active part in the conversation. Will the group be asked to make a decision? Confirm a consensus? Establish power? It's often not apparent in the official agenda.

They are also prone to stay afterward to close off the discussion and talk about other top-of-mind issues. Men viewed these pre- and post-meeting moments as significant business-building opportunities and often used this time to test their ideas and garner support.

In contrast, the authors revealed, women tend to arrive promptly for meetings, but not particularly early, so they miss the informal discussion that men find important to insight gathering. Moreover, women are much more unlikely than are men to linger after the meeting for more discussion. Instead, when the last agenda item is completed, women quickly depart for another meeting or they return to their offices to address pressing matters.

Lesson: The time before and after a meeting is critical for building alliances with attendees. In addition, these moments can be truly important to understanding what's *really* happening in a firm.

PRINCIPLE #6: PREPARE TO SPEAK SPONTANEOUSLY.

My fellow director Dr. Judith Craven is my role model regarding this principle. She has taught me to think through delicate matters before a meeting and to be judicious about when and how an issue is shared. Is the concern shared in committee? During executive session that includes only independent board members? Or is it told in confidence to another board member to gauge mutual concern? Her comments are always laced with respect for the listener.

Think ahead. Prepare *in advance* to speak spontaneously. Come to the meeting having rehearsed your salient points. Says Lynne Ford, executive vice president of Calvert Investments, a Bethesda, Maryland–based investment management firm, who was interviewed for *Break Your Own Rules*: "Even some of the casual, off-the-cuff remarks you hear have been rehearsed. If it sounds good, it was probably prepared."

I personally initiate telephone calls with one or more colleagues a few days before important board meetings. I've found it a productive way to get their opinions about the agenda items and input on any read-ahead materials we have been provided. This has proved extremely useful in organizing my pre-meeting thoughts.

Drive the conversation forward. In *Break Your Own Rules*, Anne Taylor, vice chairman and regional managing partner at Deloitte LLP, explains that experience has taught her that her impact in a meeting is maximized when she finds an opportunity to "turn it in a different and more productive direction with questions like, 'Have you thought of this . . .?' or 'What if we looked at it this way . . . ?'"

Own your opinions. When your idea or opinion energizes a conversation, the speed of the conversation accelerates and more voices join in. This is a pivotal moment. Your opinion has made it to center stage, and it's important you keep it there. *Forbes* contributor Bonnie Marcus reports that we sabotage ourselves by using weak language ("Do You Sabotage Yourself by Using Weak Language?" December 9, 2011). I've used some of Bonnie's sage advice and my own ideas in these how-to's:

Instead of: I don't know.	Use this: I'll follow up.
Instead of: I would just like to say . . .	Use this: Here is my plan.
Instead of: I want you to know . . .	Use this: I recommend . . .

Stay calm and carry on. In the *Harvard Business Review* article "Replace Meaningless Words with Meaningful Ones" (December 7, 2011), Jerry Weissman advises women to use stronger words rather than meaningless ones.

Men acknowledge the existence of a double standard: "Women have to be mindful to stay within the guardrails;

men don't," one male executive told us. Until that changes, women need to ensure that they are seen as composed and in command of their emotions. It is not so much *what* women say as *how* they say it. [Women] need to keep an even tone, not shift to a higher pitch when under duress. They need to speak deliberately and avoid signaling frustration through sarcasm or curtness.

Lesson: *How* you communicate is critical to how people perceive you. Practice. Practice. Practice.

PRINCIPLE #7: BE POLITICALLY SAVVY.

Office politics gets a bad rap. For many, it implies ruthlessness. But John Eldred, a professor at the Wharton School of the University of Pennsylvania, reminds us that politics is simply how power gets worked out in an organization on a practical, daily basis.

In *Break Your Own Rules*, authors Jill Flynn and Kathryn Heath devote a chapter to the topic of politics. Here are three principles to consider:

1. Map the "hot spots." In my board work on risk evaluation, we look at "hot" risks. In Luby's case, our restaurants on the coast of Texas are at high risk for hurricane damage. It occurs to me that this same principle holds true in ferreting out the "hot" peer groups who have influence in your organization. Knowing where the alliances are, both formally and informally, is important. In the end, you must learn whom you can trust and whose interests and concerns can help you achieve buy-in or enable you to influence a decision.

2. Interpret the numbers. The real stories are told in company financial statements. At least a week before each board meeting Luby's board members receive

an electronic "Board Book" file on our company-issued iPads. I spend time reviewing the Income Statement and Balance Sheet. I particularly pay attention to changes from quarter to quarter. These numbers tell a story: where we may be in jeopardy, what departments are performing well, where risks are increasing. Do the same with your financial statements. It will help you understand the realities of how your organization operates and how to pinpoint where board oversight is needed.

3. Be present. Practice being present in your conversations. Pay attention to what is said and how other people react to the conversation. You'll likely uncover cues and inferences that can help you understand people's needs and motives. These insights can help you identify concerns to craft "win-wins."

Lesson: Don't fear "politics." Instead, embrace the force and let it help you drive your mission.

PRINCIPLE #8: LEARN FROM SETBACKS AND FAILURE.

Learning how to "fail forward" is key to learning to lead.

Before Vera Wang became the famous fashion designer she is today, she failed to make the 1968 U.S. Olympic Figure Skating Team. With that failure, she focused on a different goal and took a job as a *Vogue* assistant, and within a year the incredibly talented assistant was promoted to senior fashion editor at age twenty-three. Fifteen years of amazing creative work followed. But she was ultimately passed over for *Vogue's* editor-in-chief position. But again she "failed forward" into the quintessential fashion designer she is today. Vera Wang still lives with the possibility of failure. As she tells *The Cut* (an online publication of *New York Magazine*) in an article titled "Vera Wang Says: Know When to Walk Away . . . and Start Something New" (June 24, 2015),

> No matter how bad things get, no matter how discouraged I feel, no matter how much of a failure I feel like—and that applies to motherhood, friendship, everything—I try to believe there's a reason, there's a process, and there's a learning experience. Maybe the journey is where I gained wisdom, where I gained confidence, a sense of reality, a sense of creativity.

Yes, let's be real here. "Failure is brutal, ugly and unpleasant," writes Costica Bradatan, professor of humanities at Texas Tech University and author of *Dying for Ideas: The Dangerous Lives of the Philosophers* (Bloomsbury Academic, 2015). "Whenever it [failure] happens, it is profoundly unsettling because it shatters your certainties; it makes you question your place in the world, your worthiness . . . Sure, failure can also lead to success later on, but before that, you have to face it now and on its own terms."

Brian Grazer's Big Failure

Iconic film and television producer Brian Grazer believes failure has been the most instructive force in his life. In a column in *WSJ. Magazine* (Soapbox, April 2015), he explains

> With my movie about a mermaid, *Splash*, I must have had a thousand people say no to me on that. And they always said no in a way that was kind of degrading, like—what, a mermaid? And so when it worked, I thought, Wow! Nobody knows. . . . So I thought you just have to follow your own truth.

My Big Failure

Because Brian Grazer was immersed in Hollywood's high-stakes games, I imagine the ridicule was hard to bear, especially since it came from successful studio heads and directors. While I can't possibly know what that level of defeat feels like, my failure was very visible among a group of people whose opinions mattered deeply to me. Here's what happened.

About three years into my career as a loyalty consultant and speaker, I lobbied hard and won a speaking slot at *Inc.* magazine's high-profile business conference. I was one of fifty-five speakers, some of whom were considered the best in the business. My seminar was filled to the brim, with some folks even standing in the back. As I spoke about how you "grow" prospects into customers and clients, I knew in my gut I was not connecting with the audience. Two weeks later it was official. *Inc.* sent out audience ratings. I came in dead last!

I was devastated. Not only did *Inc.* and I know I "stunk," all of my peers knew it too. I grieved for weeks. At my lowest point, I thought the only real solution was to close my business and go find "a real job."

Desperate for help, I reached out to my trusted confidante, friend, and speaking colleague, Jim Bearden. I laid out the facts. Jim didn't flinch. He looked me square in the eye and said in his matter-of-fact manner, "Jill, sometimes you have to take yourself to the woodshed." He went on to explain that I had to be ruthless with myself in acknowledging this poor performance and the failings it exposed.

I left our meeting with a knot the size of a baseball in the pit of my stomach. But I thought deeply about Jim's words as I drove back to my office. Upon arrival, I laid a blank sheet of paper on my desk and started listing the many ways I had let my *Inc.* audience down. Among the trespasses I listed were these:

> I revealed nothing about myself and my personal life.
> I hid behind my information.
> I wasn't entertaining.
> I gave them little to laugh about.
> I shared facts, not stories.

Using this painful-to-think-about list, I began to realize my entire presentation and speaking style needed an overhaul. Yes, I would continue to make sure my information was fresh and new, but now my goal was to go further and make my presentations touch the hearts in the audience.

Two years later, after many interim presentations, I stepped up and called my contact at *Inc.* magazine with this message: "I know I let you down, and I apologize. I've performed major surgery on my presentations. I would like you to consider me again as a speaker for your events. I have recommendation letters from many groups that you know. May I send them to you?"

There was a quiet pause, and then he shared: "Jill, your call is timely. Just last week I called some of my scouts and asked what speaker they had heard recently that they really liked. Both named you. I would welcome you to speak at an upcoming conference."

Lesson: It's ironic, but the uncertainty and grief that result from setbacks and deep failure can often inspire your best work. Moreover, failure teaches you to be humble and grounded. It gives you lessons to share with your team, and your honesty and candor will be one of the most respected virtues you'll possess as a successful leader.

RULE #9: RECRUIT SPONSORS.

A recent McKinsey study, titled "Unlocking the Full Potential of Women in the US Economy," looked at barriers women cite as factors that convince them the odds of getting ahead are too daunting. "Not having a sponsor to create opportunities" was found to be one of those major obstacles. (You might want to reread chapter 5 about networking.)

I have learned firsthand the difference between mentors and sponsors. Mentors counsel and advise you; sponsors go further. Equipped with their senior status and huge network of influential contacts, they carry your "professional flag" out into the world to help position and lobby for you for top executive positions.

Look for both men and women to sponsor you. In my experience, high-powered women are fierce advocates for other women. I continually find they know how hard the climb has been and want to help. Networking is key here. Some of my best connections have resulted from my attending the speech of a noted authority.

Here's my technique: After the presentation, approach this person near the podium. (Others will be seeking the same, so be patient and wait your turn.) Offer your business card and ask for the keynote speaker's. When you are on your computer again, go to LinkedIn and ask to connect. Remind the influencer of your recent conversation. That's one approach. Another is to e-mail the influencer directly. Persistence pays. Even if the individual doesn't respond immediately, keep reaching out. It helps to speak of commonalities and experiences you both share. (For example, you grew up in neighboring towns, share the same alma mater, etc.)

One of my favorite networking stories goes like this. Years ago, I attended an *Inc.* magazine conference at which customer relations thought-leader Don Peppers keynoted. As happens with any "famous" speaker, attendees swarmed him with questions and business cards. I purposely waited and was the last to speak him. I informed Don I was coauthoring a book on customer winback. He politely shared that he did not endorse many books. I smiled and said, "Don, I'm not asking for an endorsement. I'm so confident about what we're writing, I would like you to consider penning the foreword." He gave me his card and instructed me to send the finished manuscript along with a reminder of our conversation. Two weeks later I had a voice mail from Don saying he and his partner, Dr. Martha Rogers, would indeed write the foreword. This taught me to always go for it. The worst the person can say is no.

When looking for sponsors, consider your contacts and colleagues on boards abroad. Many countries have now set quotas for publicly held companies. Norway was the first in Europe to legislate boardroom quotas, joined by Spain, France, and Iceland. At this writing, Italy, Belgium, the Netherlands, and Germany have followed.

A vast number of American women executives have lived and worked for long periods of time abroad. If that's you, know this: These quotas can be a huge door opener in landing a seat on public boards in Europe.

My Sponsor, Joe McKinney

Joe McKinney and I joined Luby's board of directors at the same time. He chairs the Audit Committee and has deep banking experience. Joe is currently co-chair of Broadway Bank, a family-owned bank in San Antonio that is expanding throughout central Texas. He sponsored me onto Broadway's Austin Advisory board and that has enabled me to get a bird's-eye view of banking and their well-run operation.

Joe's background explains why he's such a down-to-earth, likable, and fun-to-work-with executive who wants to help others. The first in his family to attend college, he grew up with the "astronaut kids" outside of Houston. As Joe tells the story, John Glenn contacted a Harvard recruiter and said, "We have a kid here who you should look at." The recruiter visited, and Joe was offered a scholarship to play football at Harvard, alongside now well-known actor Tommy Lee Jones. From Harvard, Joe attended the Wharton Business School.

Joe is a guy who has never forgotten where he came from, and I'm grateful for his friendship and sponsorship.

Joe Mckinney (seated, fifth from left), and the Broadway Bank Advisory Board

Lesson: Sponsors are a proven link to fast-tracking your career. They will pull for you. They will throw your hat into the ring. They have the power to deliver you to your destination. Find them, forge the relationships, and perform well in the assignments you earn as a result of their sponsoring you. By doing so, you enhance their own careers and their reputations for recognizing talent.

TOOLS FOR YOUR JOURNEY

- Prize your instincts and emotional intelligence. Put them to work to lead.

- Taking leadership can feel uncomfortable. Feel the anxiety and step up and lead anyway.
- Defining your values will empower you to lead with courage.
- Opportunities are constantly lost if you wait to be recognized. Better to speak up for what you want and need.
- Leverage pre- and post-meeting moments to build and strengthen relationships.
- Prepare in advance to speak spontaneously. Come to meetings having rehearsed your important points.
- Be politically savvy by being aware of where the true power in an organization resides. Map those "hot" colleagues and get to know their interests and concerns. It helps you achieve buy-in and influence decisions.
- The uncertainty and grief that result from deep failure often inspire a person's best work.
- Recruit sponsors. Look for both senior top-level executives and sitting corporate directors who are willing to stand behind you and position you for new opportunities.
- Think globally when considering your sponsors. Quotas in European countries and other places in the world are enabling women to be seated in corporate boardrooms.

GETTING STARTED

"A woman's natural aptitude for intuition, diplomacy, and value-based decision making are critical to leadership."
—Dr. Judith Craven

Your opportunity for earning a board seat is in taking action today! Here's how:

Action #1: Test Your Readiness. Gauge your "fit" for a corporate board seat by answering a few important questions.

Action #2: Craft Your Board Search Strategy. Begin with a clear understanding of what the *board* wants, rather than what you want. (Your preferences come later.)

Action #3: Find Boards That Would Welcome You. Compile your prospect list and vet it, eliminating poor contenders. Prioritize your list, zeroing in on those for which your experience could be most useful. Share you list with trusted colleagues and ask for AIR: Advice, Insight, Recommendations.

Action #4: Attract Boards To You. Create your personal brand to draw the "right" boards. Use this success formula: Passionate Expertise + Fearless Work + Visibility + Recognition = Opportunity.

Action #5: Network with Board Directors and Influencers. Practice the Ten Rules of Networking. These include making networking friend-making, addressing people by name, and making peace with former adversaries.

Action #6: Ace Your Board Interviews. Do your homework! Prepare for three stages—Before the interview, During the interview, After the interview.

Action #7: Vet Your Board Invitations. Follow ten "best practices" to make your critical decision for joining a board.

Action #8: Women, Prepare To Lead. Practice nine "rules" to ready yourself for the corporate boardroom. These include, embracing your special gifts, not waiting for permission and recruiting sponsors.

ACKNOWLEDGMENTS

"Books may well be the only true magic."
—Alice Hoffman

Early in life I was blessed with wise, committed teachers who taught me the art of writing. My first teacher was my maternal grandmother, Ada Faircloth Marsh. "Ma-ma" was a published author, accomplished artist, talented grade school teacher, and a woman deeply devoted to God. To this day, my late grandmother is the "North Star" in my life. Why? Because she taught me the importance of character. From an early age, I played Scrabble with her, and Ma-ma wrote me a letter when I was in college in which she described the experience. She said I always insisted on "playing by the rules," and she knew I would go out into the world and play by the rules. I try to live by that rule every day.

My grade school teachers Mrs. Edna Gaddy, Mrs. Ruby Sinclair, and Mrs. Lula Eubanks drilled into me the grammar and punctuation rules I use every day. My high school English teacher, Miss Myrtle Kiker, is the reason I can write books. She taught me how to write essays and term papers. I am blessed beyond words that she crossed my path.

Book writing consultant Thorn Bacon came into my life in 1989. He taught me an invaluable lesson: Good books tell great stories. I've tried to practice that principle in every book I've written.

Talented executives and board directors have generously shared their advice and told their stories on these pages. They include John Barra, Melanie Barstad, Dr. Bill Cunningham, Dr. Judith Craven, Melissa Herkt, Jan Lehman, Gen. Don Cook, Tom Knudson, Jim Offerdahl, Janet Wright, Janet Kelly, Ralph Hasson, John Pincelli, Kevin Krone, Mel Cooper, Lori Gobillot, Mellody Hobson, Beryl Raff, Libby Sartain, Carol Brookins, Anne Ward, Don Peppers, Linda Miller, Carol B. Tome, Anne Taylor, Christine B. LaFollette, Jim Bearden, George Lake, Gail Page, Melissa Fruge, Dr. Linda Henman, and Stephanie Lucie.

I've been blessed with wonderful book mentors. They include Cheryl Rae, Karen Post, Jeanne Bliss, Kristen Friend, Ray Bard, Dennis and Suzie Welch, Lari Bishop and Alex Head of Draft LAB, Judy Barrett, Linda O'Doughda, Carol Smalley, Barbara Hendricks, Justin Esquivel, Bill Fitzpatrick, Patti DeNucci, Dr. Linda Golden, Bernadette Walter, and Mark Okamoto and Century Management.

The National Association of Corporate Board Directors has been a great source for this book's research, especially staff members Julie Pitts and Kelly Cook, who generously shared their invaluable Rolodexes.

A writer needs encouragement. I'm blessed with many who abundantly give it. They include my sister, Marsha Alexander, and family, Eleanor Chote, Margo and Juan Portillo, Peg Manley, Lisa Webb, Ann Pincelli, Suzanna Sugarman, Janis Morris, Karen Post, Bob Gutermuth, Peggy Ferraro, Susan Robinson, Margaret Sheridan, David Anderson, Janet Mullins, Laura Snell, Sarita and Dan Toma, and my Austin Dinner Club friends.

Creating training videos with Lynda.com has made me a better writer. As Lynda.com's Customer Loyalty author, I've been coached by the best: content manager, Kathe Sweeney; script coaches and video producers, including Lauren Haub and Joshua Mitchell; and the ace production teams surrounding my projects. And a special thank-you to Christina Burns whose skills rival those of any Hollywood makeup artist.

I have savored every minute as chairwoman of the Austin Convention & Visitors Bureau. ACVB president and CEO, Bob Lander, is a maestro at creating a "big" vision for a destination city and meticulously bringing it to life. (Hint: Avoid following Bob to the podium.) And thank-you to ACVB's amazing staff—each and every one the best in the business. Big thanks to my board of directors—all of whom brought wisdom to our cause—and to Austin Convention Center pros Mark Tester and Paul Barnes.

Mary Scott Nabers, Shanny Lott, Jane Hays, Nancy Ebe, Susan Benz, Sandra Useleman, Ellen Wood, Laura Kilcrease, Diana Keller, and Diana Holford are among the smartest gals in any room and they have taught me much about business (and life).

Special thanks to Broadway Bank vice chair, Joe McKinney; to Austin region president, Harvey Haverstein; and to my fellow Austin Advisory board members who teach me something new every meeting.

The Darla Moore School of Business at the University of South Carolina gave me my professional start in life and the school has a special place in my heart. Thanks to Dean Pete Brew for his academic leadership; former dean Hildy Teegen; former director of development, Jane Barghothi; Alumnus Relations ace, Mary Ruffin Childs; my fellow Board of Trustee members; and alumni Marcy Thompson and Jim Mackey, whose stories contributed to my book research.

Building my Board Search Accelerator (TM) tool required deep data on nearly 100,000 corporations. My long-time investment advisor, Century Management, came to my rescue. A special thanks to Mark Okamoto who has been my financial advisor and friend for many years. And to Arnold Van Den Berg, founder of Century Management, whose remarkable life story deserves a book of its own.

And finally, to the love of my life, Doug Glasgow, for making me laugh and opening the door to an amazing, new future.

CORPORATE BOARD RESOURCES & BIBLIOGRAPHY

Here are just a few of the hundreds of resources available to help deepen your understanding of corporate board service. Search by each of these categories and you'll find many more!

BOOKS AND ARTICLES

Baca, Marie. 2008. "Five Tactics for Landing a Board Seat." CBSNews.com, October 15, 2008.

Bakewell, Thomas, and James J. Darazsdi. 2014. *Claiming Your Place at the Boardroom Table: The Essential Handbook for Excellence in Governance and Effective Directorship.* McGraw-Hill Education.

Calderon, Nancy, and Susan Stautberg. 2014. *Women on Board: Insider Secrets to Getting on a Board and Succeeding as a Director.* Quotation Media.

Gutner, Toddi. 2006. "So You Wanna Be a Board Director." *BusinessWeek* (online), July 16, 2006.

Knight, Edward S. 2013. "Raising the Curtain on Proxy Advisers." *Wall Street Journal*, October 8, 2013.

Korn Ferry Institute. 2014. "Beyond 'if not, why not': The pathway to directorship for women in leadership." Available from Korn Ferry website.

Lagomarsino, Peter, and James Rowe. 2014. "Board Vetting in the Digital Age." *Directors & Boards*, Third Quarter 2014.

Light, D. K., and K. S. Pushor. 2006. *Into the Boardroom: How to Get Your First Seat on a Corporate Board*. Beaver's Pond Press.

Lublin, Joann S. 2014. "Female CEOs Make Room for Female Directors." *Wall Street Journal*, November 12, 2014.

Spencer Stuart. 2015. "Tips for Would-Be Directors." *Becoming a Better Leader* (online publication), June 2015.

Van Der Zon, Kim, and Martha Josephson. 2013. "The Path to the Boardroom." Egon Zehnder, The FOCUS magazine, fall 2013.

Warner, Judy. 2011. "Securing Your First Public Company Board Seat: Mission Possible." Directorship.com, April 15, 2011.

Woolley, Anita W., and Thomas W. Malone. 2011. "Defend Your Research: What Makes a Team Smarter? More Women." *Harvard Business Review*, June 2011.

Weber, Lauren. 2014. "Here's What Boards Want in Executives." *Wall Street Journal*, December 10, 2014.

UNIVERSITY-SPONSORED BOARD DIRECTOR EDUCATION PROGRAMS

Directors' Consortium. Looking for a cross-disciplinary executive program focusing on the role of directors in driving and sustaining corporate success? Faculty members from the Stanford Graduate School of Business, the Stanford Law School, the University of Chicago Booth School of Business, and the Tuck School of Business at Dartmouth combine their knowledge, research, and expertise to provide a dynamic program for aspiring, new, and experienced board members. The program provides a close-up on corporate board strategies, frameworks, and best practices.

Stanford's Directors' College. Taught inside Stanford Law School, many consider this the premier executive education program for directors and senior executives of publicly traded firms. Aspiring directors can also attend. Attendees report that it provides a balanced and thorough analysis of corporate governance, strategy, and compliance.

NON-UNIVERSITY-SPONSORED BOARD DIRECTOR EDUCATION PROGRAMS

National Association of Corporate Directors. This association provides great resources for aspiring corporate board directors. Services include education, research resources, and networking to corporate, private, and nonprofit boards.

New York Stock Exchange (NYSE) Governance Services. This company offers a range of training programs, advisory services, benchmarking analysis and scorecards, exclusive access to peer-to-peer events, and thought leadership on key governance topics for company directors and C-level executives.

PwC Corporate Governance. This firm provides director education programs to help directors further understand their roles and develop the technical knowledge needed to discharge their responsibilities effectively.

RESOURCES FOR WOMEN DIRECTOR ASPIRANTS

Women On Board® is a Catalyst initiative that operates in the United States and Canada. The agency promotes the appointment of women to corporate boards by selecting and pairing women corporate director candidates with mentors and sponsors.

Women on Boards. As of this writing, each week WOB posts between eight and fifteen paid and unpaid vacancies on boards. You need to have a paid subscription to WOB ($165/annum) to access the list. For details, visit www.womenonboards.org.au/my/profile/positions-search.

Women's Director Development Program: Kellogg Center for Executive Women. This course serves as a boot camp and gateway for women who aspire to serve on boards, as well as an aid for women looking to expand their range of directorship opportunities. You'll have access to directors and senior Kellogg School of Management faculty as they explore the roles of boards, ways to structure boards for high performance, and strategies for maximizing effectiveness as a board member.

CORPORATE DIRECTOR INSURANCE INFORMATION

The D&O Diary. This is a periodic journal containing items of interest from the world of directors and officers liability, with occasional commentary.

D&O Notebook: Directors and Officers Liability Blog. This blog's mission is to monitor and curate issues as they arise in the areas of deletions & omissions liability, insurance, and corporate governance. For more information, visit http://www.wsandco.com/about-us/news-and-events/blogs/do-blog.

Gifford and Associates. D&O Insurance white paper, February 2015.

The Importance of Personal Indemnification Agreements. Priya Cherian Huskins explains what an Indemnification Agreement is and why a director needs one.

CORPORATE BOARD ANNUAL SURVEYS

2020 Women on Boards Gender Diversity Index: 2011–2015 Progress of Women Corporate Directors by Company Size, State and Sector.

The Frederic W. Cook & Company Board Compensation Study. National Association of Corporate Directors Public Company Governance Survey.

Spencer Stuart U.S. Board Index.

BOARD SEAT READINESS AUDIT

BOARD ∗ SEAT
READINESS.

Board seat readiness is a big deal. And, as you'll recall from chapter 1, I've designed a quick audit tool to test your preparedness. You can take the quiz by simply penciling your answers in this book, or go online to BoardSeatReadiness.com.

BOARD SEAT SEARCH ACCELERATOR

BOARD * SEARCH
ACCELERATOR.

In *Earn Your Seat on a Corporate Board*, I provide you with some simple steps to take to pinpoint the boards that are your best possibilities for landing your ideal seat.

I have designed the "Board Search Accelerator" to produce fifty potential boards that meet your search specific criteria. All you do is "check a box" in these three key areas:

- Board-worthy skill sets
- Preferred industries
- Capitalization size: large-cap, mid-cap, small-cap, micro-cap

The search engine examines 94,000 public companies and the list is updated annually.

You'll get your list of fifty potential boards to explore. You'll want to vet the boards that hold the most promise and the quickest access to a board invitation. You'll consider director retirement, and whether the board is nearing a vacancy that fits your skill set. You'll want to examine diversity opportunity, and so forth.

Sound overwhelming? I can help. I'll provide you with a personal concierge to vet your top board choices and help you pinpoint just the right fit.

To learn more visit BoardSearchAccelerator.com.

MY BOARD RESUME

JILL GRIFFIN

📍 3818 Ridgelea Drive #A
   Austin, TX 78731
📠 737.484.0098
✉ jill@jillgriffin.net
🌐 jillgriffin.net

Seasoned public board director with deep expertise in building customer-driven culture.
Strong record of thought-leadership in customer loyalty, retention and win-back.

PUBLIC COMPANY BOARD SERVICE

2003 to Present   **LUBY'S, INC.**   Houston, TX
                             Independent Director

Luby's Inc. (NYSE: LUB) has core brands Luby's Cafeterias, Fuddruckers, Cheeseburger in Paradise and Luby's Culinary Services. 2015 FY sales totaled $394 million. Nine new stores opened. Aggressive expansion continues.

- **Executive Committee**
- **Chair:** Personnel & Administration Committee
- **Member:** Executive Compensation Committee
- **Member:** Nominating & Corporate Governance Committee

Key Achievements: Brought customer and staff loyalty metrics into boardroom. Focused P & A Committee on high performer retention and management succession. Sourced leading-edge technology for stores. Identified operational driver of Luby's guest satisfaction. Advocated electronic surveying and brought survey insights into P & A Committee. Proposed Fuddruckers POS system upgrades to improve dining experience. Championed rebranding of Luby's as a healthy family dining choice.

Jan 2014 to Present   **BROADWAY BANK**   San Antonio, TX

Broadway Bank has more than $3 billion in assets and operates 39 locations in South Central Texas, including locations on military installations in San Antonio.

- **Austin Advisory Board**

COMMUNITY AND CIVIC BOARD SERVICE

Present   **SOUPER BOWL OF CARING**   HOUSTON, TX
                             Board Director

Mission: Using the energy of the Super Bowl to mobilize youth in a united national effort to care for people in their local communities who are hungry and those in need.

| 2007 to Present | **AUSTIN CONVENTION & VISITORS BUREAU** | Austin, TX |
| | *Board Chair 2013-2016* | |

ACVB is the marketing and sales arm for the City of Austin.

• **Executive Committee** (2009-2013)

Key Achievements: Oversee CEO and staff of 56 in promoting Austin conventions and tourism. Achieved growth of city-wide room nights by 24% and average group size by 11% over previous year with more than half being "A" grade hotel rooms. Represented City of Austin on 2014 Inaugural British Airways flight to London. Presided at ACVB 2013-2015 Annual Travel Luncheons with record-breaking 800+ attendees.

| 2007 to Present | **UNIVERSITY OF SOUTH CAROLINA** | Columbia, SC |
| | *Moore School of Business - Board of Trustees* | |

School rated #1 by *U.S. News & World Report* 2014 rankings in graduate and undergraduate international business.

Key Achievements: Personally endowed MBA Fellowship for deserving candidates with exceptional financial need. Helped raise $90 million for new business school facility opening July 2014. Contributed thought leadership to Moore School's curriculum improvement. Recipient of 2005 Distinguished Alumni Award.

| 2007 to Present | **NAT'L ASSOC. OF CORPORATE DIRECTORS (NACD)** | Houston, TX |

Tri Cities Chapter - Board of Directors

• **Austin Membership Co-Chair** (2007-2010)
• **Austin Program Co-Chair** (2010-2014)

Key Achievements: Served on committee that drove membership and sponsorship which, in turn, created and sustained one of the only self-funded NACD chapters in the United States.

PUBLISHED BOOKS

EARN YOUR SEAT ON A CORPORATE BOARD   (March 1, 2016, Jill Griffin Books)

TAMING THE SEARCH & SWITCH CUSTOMER   (2009, Wiley/Jossey Bass)
Named "Top Business Books of 2009" by *Miami Herald.*

CUSTOMER WINBACK   (2002, Wiley/Jossey Bass)
Co-authored. Named "Top 30 Books of the Year" by Soundview Executive Book Summaries.
Adopted as learning text by Professor Linda Golden at UT McCombs School of Business.

CUSTOMER LOYALTY   (2001, Completely Revised Second Edition: Wiley/Jossey Bass)
Named in Harvard Business School's "Working Knowledge" selection. Published in seven languages.
Adopted as learning text by Professor Linda Golden at UT McCombs School of Business.

CUSTOMER LOYALTY   Paperback. (1997, Wiley/Jossey Bass)
Earned best-seller status. United States Postal Service purchased 22,000 copies for distribution to small/medium sized businesses.

CUSTOMER LOYALTY   Hard cover. (1995, Simon & Schuster)

EMPLOYMENT

1988 to present

THE LOYALTY MAKER
Fortune 500 Customer Loyalty Strategist
International Keynoter and European Conference Chair

Clients Served Include: Dell, Microsoft, Sprint, Hyatt Hotels, Toyota, Siemens, Subaru, Ford Motor Company, DFW Airport, Western Union, Raytheon Aircraft, Hewlett Packard.

Key Achievements: Recognized as early thought-leader in lifecycle loyalty modeling. Performed ground-breaking work in customer win-back, save, and switch prevention.

1988 to 1990

LECTURER
University of Texas at Austin McCombs School of Business

1985 to 1988

AMERISUITES HOTELS (AUSTIN VENTURES COMPANY)
Director of Marketing & Sales

Key Achievements: Branded the hotel concept and launched chain. Chain eventually expanded to 100 locations now known as Hyatt Place.

1979 to 1985

R.J. REYNOLDS TOBACCO COMPANY
Senior Brand Manager

Key Achievements: Rose to manage corporation's largest brand, Winston, in six short years. Recognized as one of the youngest senior brand managers in corporation's history.

EDUCATION

1977 to 1979

UNIVERSITY OF SOUTH CAROLINA, COLUMBIA
Master of Business Administration

- Awarded Graduate Fellowship and Marketing Assistantships
- Advertising Manager, *Gamecock Newspaper.*

Key Achievements: Set school record for advertising sales. Recruited and managed seven sales reps. Self-funded all grad school tuition and expenses.

1974 to 1977

UNIVERSITY OF SOUTH CAROLINA, COLUMBIA
Bachelor of Science: Business Administration

- Magna Cum Laude
- Alpha Delta Pi Sorority

INTERESTS

- Mountain biking
- Bowling
- Civil war history
- Beginner in fly-fishing
- Carolina "beach music" lover
- Avid biography reader

INDEX

A

Abstraction, 60

Accomplishments
    framing your, 54
    tying strengths to, 74

Acting the part, 58–60

Action in breeding clarity, 37–40

Adjacent industries, 25, 30, 36

Adversaries, making peace with
    former, 68

AIR (advice, insight, and
    recommendations), 24–25
    asking for, 36, 39–40

Alliances, building, 100

Always in demand board skills,
    20, 21–23, 29, 31, 36

Anecdotes, 60

Answers, care in preparing,
    75–76

Apple, 58

Art of Manliness (McKay and
    McKay), 60

Ascension, 74

Auditor independence, 11

Austin Convention & Visitors
    Bureau, 127

Automotive One, 44

B

Bain Capital, 49

Bakewell, Thomas, 27–28

Barrett, Colleen, 45

Barstad, Melanie, 33, 54–55

Bearden, Jim, 105

Beard, James, Foundation, xii

Bell, Alexander Graham, 71

Bezos, Jeff, 43

Blalock, Becky, 60, 97

Blank, Arthur, 98

Bloomberg, 20

Board climate, identifying, 72

Board literacy, xiii

Boardroom, familiarity with, 78

Board seat concentration, 30

Board Seat Readiness Audit,
    9–16, 121

Board Seat Search Accelerator,
    35, 121–122

Body language, 59–60

Book, writing a, 48–50

Boys Clubs, xii

Bradatan, Costica, 104

Bradley, Bill, 27

Branding tools
    acting the part as, 58–60
    crafting resume as, 52–55
    elevator pitch as, 56
    first impressions as, 57–58
    speaking and writing the
        part, 60–62

Brand managers, 95

Break Your Own Rules: How

to Change the Patterns of Thinking That Block Women's Paths to Power (Flynn et al.), 99–101

Briefcase, in making first impression, 58

Bristow Group, 26

Brookins, Carole, 47

C

Calendar, in vetting board invitations, 83–84

Calm, staying, 101–102
in corporate interview, 78

Calvert Investments, 100

Capitalization size of public companies, 3, 27

Career experience, 25

Car, in making first impression, 58

Carnegie, Dale, 63

Catalyst Executive Women in Foodservice, xii

Change, synchronizing vision and values to drive, 96–98

Cheerleading, refraining from, 78

Chin, Carolyn, 56

Cintas, 33, 54–55

Claiming Your Place at the Boardroom Table (Bakewell and Darazsdi), 27

Clarity, action in breeding, 37–40

Clark, Dorie, 50

Clothes, in making first impression, 58

Clubbiness, 85

Coherence, in writing, 61

Collective intelligence, 5

Colonial First State, 35

Columbus, Christopher, 47

Comfort zone, pushing oneself out of, 95

Communication, through storytelling, 60

Compensation, for service on corporate board, 10

Contacts game, 64, 69

Contacts, reaching out to, 73–74

Continental Airlines, 26

Conversation, driving forward, 101

Cook, Frederick W., & Company Board Compensation Study, 3, 120

Cool, staying in corporate interview, 78

Cooper, Mel, 61

Core strengths, 31

Corner, avoiding painting yourself into, 75

Corporate board(s)
apparentness of fit, 33
attracting to you, 43–62
case studies of, 29–32
compensation for service on, 10
contacts of directors on, 12–13
crafting search strategy for, 19–36
decisions to set strategy, 24–28
declining invitation to join, 88
demand of service on, 17
earning seat on, 111–112
establishing board-worthy skills, 33–35
exiting early, 86
finding welcoming, 37–41
functions of, 2–3

importance of attendance, 83
individuals on, 2
invitation to join, 6
involvement of family, friends, mentors and, 17
kinds of, 19–20
legal duties of, 2
liability of, 10–11
reasons for serving on, xvi–xvii, 1–7
resources for, 117–122
sample agenda for, 4–5
sizes of, 72–73
strategic planning for, 34–35
testing readiness to serve on, 9–17
time needed to serve on, 10
turnover on, 6
women on, 5, 91–93
Corporate board annual surveys, 120
Corporate board interviews, 71–82
(*See also* Corporate board interviews, preparation for)
asking questions in, 77–80
being forthcoming in, 78
refraining from cheerleading, 79
staying calm and cool in, 79
storytelling in, 79
thinking strategically in, 79–80
seeking feedback during or after, 81
sending note of gratitude, 81
Corporate board interviews, preparation for, 72–77
(*See also* Corporate board interviews)
avoid painting yourself in corner, 75
being prepared for broad range of topics, 75
as distinguished from job interviews, 73
doing homework for, 72–73
expecting vetting in, 76–77
logistics in, 72
picking references with care, 73
Corporate board invitations, 83–89
calendar in, 83–84
clubbiness in, 85
declining, 88
evaluating risk through insider interviews, 86
feeling passion in, 86
investigating director insurance, 87
lawsuits and, 87
research in, 85
staying open-minded in, 87–88
trust-ability in, 84–85, 88
Corporate board skills buckets
always in demand skills, 20, 21–23, 29, 31, 36
subject matter skills, 20, 24, 29, 36
Corporate director insurance information, 120
Corporate governance, 11
Cox Enterprises, 20
Craven, Judith, 77, 91, 100, 111
Cuddy, Amy, 59
Customer loyalty
building case for, 49, 50
importance of, 49

writing book on, 48
Customer Loyalty: How to Earn It, How to Keep It, 49, 50, 51, 128
Customer Winback, 50, 128
Customization, 54–56
CV, 51. See also Resume

D

Darazsdi, James J., 27–28
Dare: Straight Talk on Confidence, Courage, and Career for Women in Charge (Blalock), 60, 97
Declining, corporate invitations, 88
Defacto power, 1
Dell Computer, 20
Dell, Michael, 20
Deloitte LLP, 101
DeNucci, Patti, xv
Depreciation, 13
Derivative action, 87
Dickens, Charles, 83
Differences
    embracing power of your, 50–51
Differences, buying, versus similarities, 77
Director insurance, investigating, 87, 88, 120
Directors' Consortium, 118
Dodd Frank Act, xii
D&O Diary, 120
D&O Notebook: Directors and Officers Liability Blog, 120
Dugan, Jimmy, 35
Duke Power, 56
Dying for Ideas: The Dangerous Lives of the Philosophers, 104
Dysart, Theodore, 85

E

Egon Zehnder International, Inc., 72
Eldred, John, 102
Elevator pitch, 56
Ely, Robin J., 93
E-mail, 61
Emerson, Arthur, 58
Emily Post's Etiquette, 60
Emotional intelligence, 94, 109
Employee compensation, health insurance as part of, 45
Enhanced financial disclosure, 11
Enron scandal, 11, 12, 85
Entrepreneur, thinking like a, 11
Ernst & Young, 14
Executive suite, striving for the, 35
Expertise, making undeniable, 51
Eye contact, making, 59

F

Face-to-face interviews, 72
Facial cues, 61
Failure, learning from, 103–106
Fearless work, 44–46
Feedback
    in networking, 68
    seeking, from corporate interview, 81
Financial literacy, 12
First impressions, 57–58
    briefcase in, 58
    car in, 58
    clothes in, 58
    grooming in, 58
    jewelry in, 58
    in networking, 67
    pen in, 58
Flexibility, 40
Flexigroup Limited, 35

Flynn, Jill, 99
Ford, 19
Ford, Lynne, 100
For-profit private board experience, seeking out, 34
Forthcoming, being, 78
Franklin, Benjamin, 9
Fraud, 87
Friends, making, in networking, 64, 69

G

Gay and lesbian employees, offering of benefits to, 45
GE, 19
Generous skeptic, 15
Gibran, Khalil, 1
Gifford and Associates, 120
Girls Clubs, xii
Glenn, John, 108–109
Gobillot, Lori, 26, 28
Godin, Seth, 15, 43
Google, 19, 55
Goonewardene, Julie, 53
Go to person, building brand as, 65
Gratitude, sending note of, 81
Gray, Scott, 12
Grazer, Brian, 104
Grids, 40, 41
Griffin, Jill, 127–128
    board resume of, 123–126
Grooming, in making first impression, 58
Gutermuth, Bob, 2

H

Hands, shaking, 59
Hasson, Ralph, 15–16, 64
Health insurance, 45
Health, Kathryn, 99

Heidrick & Struggles' Global Board of Directors Practice, 85
Heinz, HJ, 20
Helpfulness, 57
Helzberg Diamonds, 44
Henman, Linda, 57
Hernandez, Keith, 95
Herres, Robert, 50, 84
The Hill (web post), 13
Hobson, Mellody, 27–28
Holt, Mary Davis, 99
HomeAway, Inc., 23
Home Depot, 97, 98
Homework, doing your, 14, 85
    for interviews, 72
Horn, Carolyn, 57
Hot spots, mapping the, 102, 110
Houston Women's Chamber of Commerce, 35
Humor, power of, 13
Huskins, Cherian, 120
Hyatt Place, 48

I

Ibarra, Herminia, 93
Indemnification agreements, 120
In-depth analysis, 14
Inside directors, 22
Insider interviews, evaluating risk through, 86
Insight, digging for, 14
Instincts, prizing your, 109
Insurance
    director, 87, 88, 120
    health, 45
    self, 45
Intellectual acuity, showing, 61
Intelligence, emotional, 94, 109

Internal control assessment, 11
Interviews. See also Corporate
	board interviews
		evaluating risk through
			"insider," 86
		job, 73
Invitation, declining, to join
	corporate board, 88

J

Jargon, 43
Jarrett, Valerie, 98–99
JCPenney, 44
JD Powers customer satisfaction
	ratings, 49
Jewelry, in making first
	impression, 58
Jo-Ann Fabric and Craft Stores,
	44
Job interviews, 73
Jobs, Steve, 58
Johnson & Johnson, 33, 55
Johnson, Lady Bird, 65
Josephson, Martha, 72

K

Kennedy, John F., 13–14
Kennedy, Robert, 13–14
Kindness, 57
Kindnesses, 57, 65
Knowledge, sharing your, 51–52
Kohlberg Kravis Roberts and
	Co., xi, xii
Kolb, Deborah, 93
Korn/Ferry International, 34
Krone, Kevin, 23

L

Lagomarsino, Peter, 55
Large-caps, 3, 27
	board size for, 73

Lawsuits, research on, 87
Leadership muscle, 93
Leadership, value-driven, 97–98
Leaders, women as, 93–110
A League of Their Own, 35
Lehman, Jan, 19
Leveraging meeting time, 99–100
Liability of board service, 10–11
Linked In, 107, 127
Lists
	compiling your, 38, 41
	eliminating poor contenders,
		38–39
	prioritizing your, 39
	vetting your, 38, 41
Logistics, knowing, for
	interviews, 72
Lone vote, casting the, 15–16
The Loyalty Effect (Reichheld),
	49
Luby's/Fuddruckers, Inc., xvi, 50,
	58, 76, 77, 84, 87, 127
	board buddy system of, 12
	use of leading-edge
		technology by, 13
Lynda.com, 127

M

Macy's, 44
Mader, Steve, 34
Malone, Thomas W., 5
Manners, practicing good, 60
Marcus, Bernie, 98, 101
Marketability, broadening of, 46
Marketing awareness, 49
McCombs, Red, 49–50
McKay, Brett, 60
McKay, Kate, 60
McKinney, Joe, 108–109
Meeting time, leveraging,
	99–100

Mentors, differences between
    sponsors and, 107
Mentorship, 11, 12
MGP Ingredients, 47–48
Micro-caps, 3, 27, 28, 36
    board size for, 73
Microsoft, 19
Mid-caps, 3, 27, 28
    board size for, 73
Miller, Linda, 47–48
Mini-networks, 67
Mintz Group, 55
Miyake, Issey, 58
Mobile/cell phone, turning off,
    59
Morris, Edna, xiv
Muir, Gaspar, 84

N

Name, addressing people by, 65,
    69
Nasdaq, 20
National Association of
    Corporate Directors, 118
National Association of Public
    Company Governance Survey,
    3, 6, 72–73
Nervousness, 60
Networking, 12–13, 63–69, 107
    addressing people by name
        in, 65, 69
    building, 51
    cautiousness in, 68
    feedback in, 68
    first impressions in, 67
    framing "ask" in, 68, 69
    friend making in, 64, 69
    kindnesses in, 65, 69
    making it personal, 66–67,
        69
    making peace with

    adversaries in, 58
    mini-networks in, 67
    as numbers and contacts
        game, 64, 69
    saying "yes" in, 67
    thinking function in, 66, 69
    warm-up questions in, 66,
        69
New York Stock Exchange, 20
    Governance Services, 119
No, casting lone vote of, 15–16
Non-compete clauses, 32
Non-for-profit opportunities, 34
Non-university sponsored board
    director education programs,
    118–119
Note of gratitude, sending, 81
Numbers game, 64, 69
Numbers, interpreting the,
    102–103

O

Obama, Barrack, 98–99
Onboard Boot Camp, 56
Online searches, 85
Open-minded, staying, 87–88,
    89
Opinions, owning own, 101
Optimistic mindset, 14–15
Outside directors, 22

P

Pappas, Chris, 88
Pappas, Harris, 88
Passionate expertise, 44
Passion, feeling the, 86, 89
Peace, making with former
    adversaries, 68
Pen, in making first impression,
    58
People, addressing, by name, 65,

69
Peppers, Don, 107–108
Permission, not waiting for,
    94–96
Personal brand, 43–52
    fearless work in, 44–46
    passionate expertise in, 44
    recognition in, 48–52
    visibility in, 46–48
Personal, making it, 66–67
Pincelli, John, 63
Political savviness, 102–103, 110
Porter, Michael, 19
Positioning: The Battle for Your
    Mind (Ries and Trout), 47
Post, Anna, 60
Post, Peggy, 60
Present, being, 103
Private corporations, 20
Privatization, 20
Productive conflict, xvi
Professionalism, 57
Proof of commitment, for gay
    and lesbian employees, 45
Proxies, granting of, 1
Public corporations, 19–20
    capitalization size of, 3
    types of directors, 22
Publix Super Markets, 20
PwC Corporate Governance, 119

Q
Questions
    asking, in corporate
        interview, 79–80
    framing of, 68, 69
    warm-up, 66, 69

R
Raff, Beryl, 44
Reaching out, 53

Readiness, testing, to serve on
    corporate board, 9–17
Reading, 61
Recognition, 48–52
References, picking, for
    interviews, 73
Reichheld, Fred, 49
Research, 85
    on lawsuits, 87
Respect in determining trust-
    ability, 84–85
Resume
    crafting of, 52–55
    double-checking, for
        accuracy, 55
    of Griffin, Jill, 123–126
Resume writers, searching
    experienced, 54
Reynolds, R. J., Tobacco
    Company, 48, 127
Ries, Al, 47
Risk, evaluating, through
    "insider" interviews, 86
RJ Gold, 95
RJR Tobacco Company, 94, 95
Rogers, Martha, 108
Romweber, Jane, xi, xii–xiii
Rowe, James, 55

S
Sarbanes-Oxley Act (2002), 11
Sartain, Libby, 44–46
Self-assessment, 53
Self-insurance, 45
Sensitive topics, speaking up
    about, 15
Setbacks, learning from, 103–106
Shareholder votes, 1
Skill set, broadening of, 46
Small-caps, 3, 27, 28, 36
    board size for, 73

Smiling, 59

Social media profiles, editing your, 55

Solo, going, 53

Souper Bowl of Caring, 128

South Carolina, University of, Daniel Management Center, xii

Southwest Airlines, 23, 44–46

Speaking up, 98–99
  on sensitive topics, 15

Speaking voice, controlling your, 60–61

Sponsors
  differences between mentors and, 107
  recruiting, 106–109, 110

Stanford's Directors' College, 118

Stautberg, Susan, 56

Storytelling
  communicating through, 60
  in corporate board interviews, 78

Strengths
  prioritizing, 74
  tying to accomplishments, 74

Stuart, Spencer, U.S., Board Index, 3, 6, 120

Stuart, Stuart, 79

Subject matter board skills, 20, 24, 29, 35, 36

Sysco, 77

T

Taming the Search-and-Switch Customer: Earning Customer Loyalty in a Compulsion-to-Compare World, 128

Taylor, Anne, 101

Team player, being a, 14

TEDGlobal Talk, 59

10-K reports, 87

10-Q reports, 87

Terra Industries, 47

Text messages, 61

Thinking function, 66, 69

3M, 11

Time, needed to serve on corporate board, 10

Timing, as always in demand skill, 23

Tome, Carol B., 97

Tractor Supply Company, xi, xii, xiii

Traywick, Mabel, 57

Tri-Cities Chapter of the National Association or Corporate Directors, 35

Trout, Jack, 47

Trust-ability, 88
  respect in determining, 84–85

Trust, but verify attitude, 76

Turley, James S., 14

U

United Services Auto Association, 50

University-sponsored board director education programs, 118

V

Value-driven leadership, 97–98

Values
  defining, 110
  synchronizing, to drive change, 96–98

Van Der Zon, Kim, 72

Vespucci, Amerigo, 47

Vetting
    expecting deep, 76
    preparing for lengthy
        process, 76–77
Vinson & Elkins, 26
Visibility, 46–48
    costs for lack of, 47
Vision, synchronizing, to drive
    change, 96–98
Voice, controlling your speaking,
    60–61

W

Walters, Barbara, 66
Wang, Vera, 103–104
Ward, Anne, 34, 53
Warm-up questions, 66, 69
Washington, George, 50
Weissman, Jerry, 101–102
Women
    as advocates for other
        women, 107
    being politically savvy,
        102–103
    on corporate boards, 5,
        91–93
    embracing special gifts, 94
    as leaders, 93–110
    learning from setbacks and
        failure, 103–106
    leveraging meeting time
        and, 99–100
    natural aptitude for
        intuition, diplomacy,and
        decision making, 111
    preparing to speak
        spontaneously, 100–102
    recruiting sponsors, 106–
        109
    resources for, 119–120
    speaking up and, 98–99
    synchrronizing vision and

    values to drive change,
        96–98
    waiting for permission and,
        94–96
Women On Board, 119
Women on Boards, 119
    Gender Diversity Index,
        92–93, 120
Women's Director Development
    Programs: Kellogg Center for
    Executive Women, 119–120
Women's Foodservice Forum, xii
Woolley, Anita, 5
Words, importance of, 53
WorldCom scandal, 11
World Perspectives Inc., 47
Writing, coherence in, 61

Y

"Yes," saying, 67
YWCAs, xii

Z

Zoos Victoria, 35

ABOUT THE AUTHOR

Jill Griffin is an independent public board director, an internationally published, Harvard "Working Knowledge" author, a global thought leader on customer and staff loyalty. She is the Customer Loyalty Author for the popular training site Lynda.com, now part of the LinkedIn family.

Since 2003, Jill has served as board director for Luby's/Fuddruckers restaurants (NYSE: LUB). She chairs the Personnel & Administration committee with oversight for store operations, human resources, marketing/social media, information technology, and management compensation and succession.

Jill is a founding member of the National Association of Board Directors' (NACD) Texas Tri-Cities chapter and sits on its board of directors.

Jill holds her BS (magna cum laude) from the University of South Carolina and her MBA from USC's Darla Moore School of Business. She is the recipient of the 2005 Distinguished Alumna Award and is a member of the Darla Moore School's board of trustees.

Jill began her career in brand management in 1977 at R.J. Reynolds, where she rose in six short years to manage the corporation's largest brand, Winston.

Since 2013, Jill has served as chairwoman of the Austin Convention & Visitors Bureau. (ACVB is the "marketing and sales arm" for the City of Austin and is entrusted with bringing conventions and visitors to the "Live Music Capital of the World.") She sits on the board of directors for the Houston-based Souper Bowl of Caring whose mission is to mobilize youth nationally to care for people who are hungry and in need.

Launching her marketing consulting firm in 1988, Jill saw early the trend toward customer and employee loyalty. Her groundbreaking book, *Customer Loyalty* (Wiley, 1995, 1997, 2002; Jossey-Bass 2007), has been published in seven languages. The US Postal Service purchased 22,000 books and mailed them to businesses to help teach them direct mail techniques. Two awarding-winning books followed: *Customer Winback: How to Recapture Lost Customers—And Keep Them Loyal* (coauthored; Jossey-Bass, 2001) and *Taming the Search-and-Switch Customer: Earning Customer Loyalty in a Compulsion-to-Compare World* (Jossey-Bass, 2009).

She has always pulled for the "every-man" and this book is meant to exemplify that principle.

Jill's hobbies include mountain biking, bowling, Civil War history, travel, and Southern "Beach Music." Raised in the Carolinas, Jill lives in Austin, Texas.